Second Edition

Brain-Friendly Strategies

for
Developing
Student
Writing
Skills

Brain-Friendly Strategies

for

Developing Student

Writing

Skills

Second Edition of
Write Brain Write

Anne Hanson

CORWIN PRESS
A SAGE Company

For information:

Corwin Press
A SAGE Company
2455 Teller Road
Thousand Oaks, California 91320
www.corwinpress.com

SAGE Ltd.
1 Oliver's Yard
55 City Road
London, EC1Y 1SP
United Kingdom

SAGE India Pvt. Ltd.
B 1/I 1 Mohan Cooperative
  Industrial Area
Mathura Road, New Delhi 110 044
India

SAGE Asia-Pacific Pte. Ltd.
33 Pekin Street #02–01
Far East Square
Singapore 048763

Printed in the United States of America.

Library of Congress Cataloging-in-Publication Data

Hanson, Anne, 1950-
 Brain-friendly strategies for developing student writing skills /
Anne Hanson. – 2nd ed.
    p. cm.
 Rev. ed. of: Write brain write. Brain Store. c2002.
 Includes bibliographical references and index.
 ISBN 978-1-4129-6349-7 (cloth)—ISBN 978-1-4129-6350-3 (pbk.)
 1. English language—Composition and exercises—Study and teaching
(Elementary) 2. English language—Composition and exercises—Study and
teaching (Middle school) 3. Cognitive styles in children. I. Hanson,
Anne, 1950- Write brain write. II. Title.

 LB1576.H236 2009
 372.62'3–dc22

2008031920

This book is printed on acid-free paper.

08 09 10 11 12 10 9 8 7 6 5 4 3 2 1

Acquisitions Editor: Cathy Hernandez
Associate Editor: Megan Bedell
Production Editor: Appingo Publishing Services
Cover Designer: Karine Hovsepian

Contents

Preface

Four letters prompted the writing of this second edition: N-C-L-B.

Since the launching of the No Child Left Behind Act of 2001, federally mandated high-stakes testing has changed classroom environments across the nation, unfortunately, not for the better. District leaders, rightfully worried about the federal sanctions and stigmatizing achievement labels associated with high-stakes testing results, continue to make decisions based on raising test scores—no matter the consequences—and dismiss student-centered, brain-centered classrooms as pre-NCLB luxuries. One leader, while discussing a book on the *collateral damage* (Berliner & Nichols, 2007) brought about by the federal legislation, quipped: "That's all well and good, but what does it have to do with student achievement?"

Several years researching teacher dissatisfaction and the cognitively debilitating syndrome of teacher burnout have helped me realize teachers needed a book that would help them *defend* student-centered, brain-friendly practices against intrusive, prepackaged promises. To be taken seriously, I knew that book would need to connect brain-compatible dots with student achievement dots.

This second edition connects the dots.

The book features an original *brain-compatible framework for student achievement* that illustrates the harmony between the first edition's brain-compatible classroom principles related to safety, respect, novelty, and memory and research-based propositions and features related to student achievement, achievement that occurred in diverse settings, from rural to suburban and from middle class to below the poverty line. By connecting the dots to student achievement, the framework provides teachers evidence they need to defend their brain-centered practices against the test-centered practices being forced upon them.

WHAT'S NEW IN THE SECOND EDITION

- The brain-compatible framework for student achievement and its research-based support base

  1. *National Board for Professional Teaching Standards*: five core propositions related to standards for what accomplished teachers should know and be able to do

  2. *National Research Center on English Learning and Achievement:* six features of effective instruction

- A section on the learning brain, which provides information intended to help teachers share with their students how the amazing brain learns
- Chapters organized around six research-based features of effective instruction that fostered student achievement

  1. Teachers make connections across instruction, curriculum, and life.

  2. Students learn skills in multiple lesson types.

  3. Teachers integrate test preparation into instruction.

  4. Students learn strategies for doing the work.

  5. Students are expected to be generative thinkers.

  6. Classrooms foster cognitive collaboration.

Each of these chapters

- describes characteristics of one of the six research-based features of effective instruction and provides examples of what the feature looks like in classrooms;
- demonstrates the compatibility of the feature to brain-compatible principles from the first edition as well as to core propositions of the National Board for Professional Teaching Standards;
- presents lessons, ideas, and activities exemplifying the specific feature of the brain-compatible framework in action;
- concludes with questions related to the chapter's content.

A concluding chapter summarizes key points about the brain-compatible framework for student achievement and reflects on the vision of high-stakes testing environments with every child a lifelong learner.

OTHER VALUABLE ADDITIONS

I am grateful to the reviewers whose insights and suggestions led to other valuable additions:

- More stories from the classroom;
- More cross-curricular writing activities;
- More activities for each grade span, that is, elementary, middle, and high school easily identified in boxes titled *Calling All Teachers!;*
- More discussion of brain-compatible classroom practices in relation to diverse student populations, for example, English language learners.

WHO SHOULD READ THIS BOOK

Besides language arts teachers, I believe the second edition will be of particular use to teachers who

- believe in cross-curricular writing;
- want reputable and reliable research findings to support their brain-friendly instructional practices against teach-to-the-test practices;
- want to learn more about the research-based features of instruction that foster student achievement.

Effective instruction that advances the achievement of literacy requires safe and engaging learning environments that are more likely to occur when teachers have the support necessary to create, sustain, and defend those environments. As teacher-researchers, we must not read research and interpret it hastily. Notwithstanding, in the age of high-stakes testing where teachers are forced to replace best practice with test practice, I believe we must seize research on student achievement that suggests harmony with brain-compatible principles and run with it! We can take comfort knowing that even while we rely on research related to higher test scores, we know we are really defending what we truly believe in: brain-friendly teaching.

I hope teachers and administrators who believe in brain-compatible learning, who believe that children cannot and must not be standardized, will find support inside these pages.

Acknowledgments

My sincere thanks to the teachers and students whose inspiration and cooperation helped make this second edition possible, especially Suzanne Armstrong, Christine Hawes, Crista Guess, Pat LaCorte, Denyse Marsh, Corinne Mundy, Jim Welch, Janet Vickers, and Melissa Weger.

PUBLISHER'S ACKNOWLEDGMENTS

Corwin Press gratefully acknowledges the contributions of the following individuals:

Michael Ice, Third-Grade Teacher
Sanders Elementary School, Louisville, KY

Deborah Johnston, Eighth-Grade English Teacher
Prairie Middle School, Aurora, CO

Mary Moore, Third-Grade Teacher
Jason Lee Elementary School, Richland, WA

Sandra Ness, Ninth- and Tenth-Grade English Teacher
Patrick Henry High School, Minneapolis, MN

Wanda Stuckey, Twelfth-Grade English Teacher
Griffin High School, Griffin, GA

About the Author

Anne Hanson is a doctor of educational leadership whose research study dealt with the psychological syndrome of burnout in the No Child Left Behind's high-stakes testing workplace. A National Board-certified language arts teacher with twenty years experience, Hanson is a peer evaluator, recognized staff developer, and writing coach for teachers and students. Besides the first edition of this book, *Write Brain Write* (Corwin Press, 2002), Anne is the author of *Visual Writing*; the entry titled "Writing" in *The Praeger Handbook of Learning and the Brain*; *Wanted: Teachers for National Board Certification;* and *Thin Veils,* a novel about deadly dieting.

Hanson's awards and recognitions include Arizona Teacher of the Year finalist; Scottsdale Middle School Teacher of the Year; Japan Fulbright Memorial Fund scholar; New York Council for the Humanities scholar; and Arizona State University Martin Luther King, Jr., Spirit Award. Anne's passion for teacher and student advocacy has guided her to serve as teacher advocate and grievance representative for more than fifteen years. Advocacy has also influenced the design of her workshops, which are as diverse as her audiences, who range from administrators and teachers to parents and students. Topics include teacher and student burnout, high-stakes testing issues facing today's students, and writing strategies for teachers and students of all ages.

1 Introducing the Brain-Compatible Framework for Student Achievement

The educator cannot start with knowledge already organized and proceed to ladle it out in doses.
—John Dewey, *Experience and Education*

I have always believed that students of brain-compatible teachers who understand how the brain learns stand a greater chance to achieve on high-stakes tests—and to learn. I set out to find research to help me design a conceptual model that would demonstrate the likelihood that brain-compatible classroom practices indeed advanced student achievement. I chose reputable sources: the five core propositions of the National Board for Professional Teaching Standards (NBPTS, 2007) and the six features of effective instruction identified in Judith Langer's research (2000) conducted by National Research Center on English Language and Achievement.

The five propositions and six features interface elegantly with the four brain-compatible classroom principles I introduced in the first edition of my book and reiterate in the second. The brain-compatible framework for student achievement will help teachers protect and defend the brain-friendly practices they use to develop the writer within each one of their high-stakes-tested students. The first part of the model relates to my four brain-compatible classroom principles.

● 1

FOUR BRAIN-COMPATIBLE CLASSROOM PRINCIPLES

SAFETY. The classroom must be a safe, caring, and trusting environment before learning can take place.

RESPECT. Children flourish when their unique combination of learning styles is respected and encouraged.

NOVELTY. Interesting, novel, and challenging activities create positive emotional states that promote engagement and genuine learning opportunities.

MEMORY. Tapping into and building on existing memories influences genuine learning and nourishes new lifelong memories.

These four brain-compatible classroom principles, which I use to define brain-friendly writing environments, enhance learning across curricula at all levels of instruction from early childhood to young adulthood. If you agree with their tenets, you are likely brain-friendly teachers who care about students and know instinctively how to help students learn. In the twenty-first century's high-stakes testing environment, we need evidence beyond our instincts if we are to successfully defend brain-friendly practices against the test-prep packages forced upon us by administrators pressured to raise test scores. We need evidence that illustrates brain-compatible principles related to safety, respect, novelty, and memory align with reputable research related to student achievement. The second part of the brain-compatible framework for student achievement consists of the five core propositions of the National Board for Professional Teaching Standards (NBPTS, 2007), which provides such evidence.

FIVE CORE PROPOSITIONS OF ACCOMPLISHED TEACHING

No matter the certification area a teacher pursues, all candidates for National Board Certified Teacher (NBCT) certificates must successfully demonstrate how their teaching practices satisfy tenets grounded in five core propositions that distinguish them as *accomplished* teachers. Since 1987, only 55,000 teachers have earned National Board Certification (NBC). Clearly, the standards are high. Here are the five core propositions that represent the NBPTS policy statement (NBPTS, 2007) on what accomplished teachers *should know and be able to do*:

- Teachers are committed to students and their learning.
- Teachers know the subjects they teach and how to teach those subjects to students.
- Teachers are responsible for managing and monitoring student learning.
- Teachers think systematically about their practice and learn from experience.
- Teachers are members of learning communities.

National Board Certified Teachers (NBCTs) are not only certified, accomplished teachers but also teachers whose students perform well on high-stakes tests. Findings (e.g., Cavalluzzo, 2004; Goldhaber, 2004; Smith, 2005; Vandevoort, 2004) have shown that students of NBCTs do better on standardized tests than do students of teachers who are not NBCTs. Of note are the Goldhaber study, which involved the achievement of minority students, and the Vandevoort study, which involved the achievement of minority and special-needs students. The research findings strengthened my decision to associate brain-compatible classroom principles with NBPTS core propositions. Research findings from the National Research Center on English Language & Achievement provided another critical component of my framework designed to help brain-compatible teachers defend their instructional practices.

SIX FEATURES OF EFFECTIVE INSTRUCTION

The six features of effective instruction are based on a five-year study (Langer, 2000, 2004) reported by the National Research Center on English Language & Achievement. The study took place in four states and eighty-eight classes in twenty-two middle and high schools that were demographically comparable, from rural to suburban and middle class to urban poor. Though the research was observational versus causal, findings identified six instructional features used by effective teachers in schools where student achievement in reading and writing were higher than they were in typically performing schools. To identify effective instruction, the study looked for features that reflected much more than the current "back to the basics" notions of literacy (where passing tests somehow means proficiency). The features reflected "high literacy" (Langer, 2000) that

> refers to understanding how reading, writing, language, content, and social appropriateness work together and using this knowledge in effective ways. It is reflected in students' ability to engage in thoughtful reading, writing, and discussion about con-

tent in the classroom, to put their knowledge and skills to use in new situations and to perform well on reading and writing assessments including high stakes testing. (p. 1)

Readers familiar with brain-friendly approaches to teaching will appreciate the similarity between the six discrete features of effective instruction fostering student achievement and brain-friendly teaching practices.

1. Successful teachers make connections across instruction, curriclum, and life.

2. Students learn skills in multiple lesson types.

3. Successful teachers integrate test preparation into instruction.

4. Students learn strategies for doing the work.

5. Students are expected to be generative thinkers.

6. Classrooms foster cognitive collaboration.

THE BRAIN-COMPATIBLE FRAMEWORK FOR STUDENT ACHIEVEMENT

Concentric circles in the framework (see Figure 1.1) depict the harmony I believe exists among the four core principles of brain-compatible classrooms, the five core propositions of accomplished teaching, and the six features of effective instruction delivered by *effective* teachers. As you read, you will discover how the research-based brain-compatible framework for student achievement will help convince those who would have you use teach-to-the-test practices that the brain (indeed) matters in the classroom.

A BRAIN JOURNEY

The action research that occurs in our classrooms daily is something in which teachers can take pride. The lessons we try, the risks we take, all in the name of our students and their progress, confirm we are teacher-researchers who, ultimately, can become the accomplished teachers (NBPTS, 2007) and effective teachers (Langer, 2000, 2004) that research suggests make the difference in student achievement. As brain-compatible teacher-researchers, we owe it to ourselves to share with students some of the amazing aspects of the learning brain (Blodget, 2007; Caskey & Ruben, 2003). By sharing with students how the brain learns, we share with them that we know our actions, words, and deeds influence the extent to which authentic learning takes place.

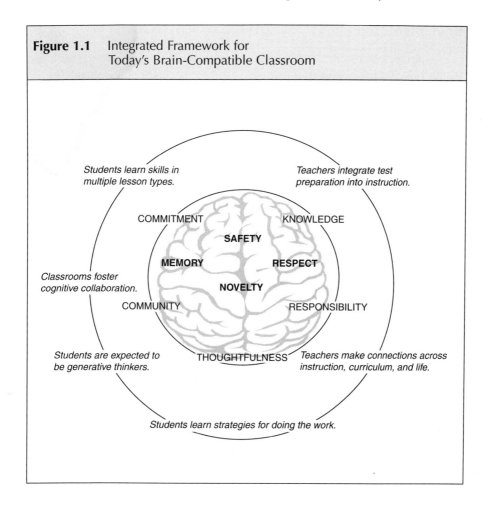

Figure 1.1 Integrated Framework for Today's Brain-Compatible Classroom

Writing on the brain's plasticity and ability to self-repair, Ross (2006) contended educators, like therapists, can make a difference in helping students scarred by negative school experiences restore their faith in teachers, themselves, and learning. Ross's work punctuated the importance of remembering we teachers should do no harm to the learning brain. Let's review brain basics to generate ideas about what we might want to share with our students to help them understand how they think and how they learn.

As a language arts teacher, I start my year by introducing students to me, their curriculum, and to my belief in brain-compatible learning. The brain journey that follows represents the parts and characteristics of the brain I have found most useful to share with my young writers. The journey helps me explain and recommit myself to my four brain-compatible classroom principles of safety, respect, novelty, and memory. The journey lays the foundation for my entire year, so let the journey begin!

Brain Stem

Imagine we are climbing up and through our spinal column. The brain inside our skull is connected to every part of the body through the spinal cord protected within our spinal column. Our climb up the spinal cord finds us meeting the *brain stem* (see Figure 1.2). The brain stem is the area of the brain in charge of monitoring vital bodily systems, such as the respiratory, circulatory, and digestive systems. The brain stem also is the site of the *reticular activating system* (RAS), which filters information, interprets it as important and worth paying attention to, or *not* worth paying attention to. We may want to share with students our realization that lessons that are interesting and engaging—that is, fun—stand a greater chance of getting noticed by the RAS than do boring test-prep lessons. However, there are ways to make high-stakes test preparation engaging enough to get the "pay attention" green light from the RAS, as we will discover in Chapter 2.

Cerebellum

As we continue our climb from the brain stem, we encounter the *cerebellum*. This tiny area comprises a tenth of the brain's weight yet houses more neurons than the rest of the entire brain! Once thought to be responsible solely for movement and coordination, the cerebellum is actually involved in cognitive processes as well. Besides helping us walk, jump, drive, and otherwise move, functionality of the cerebellum enables us to visualize our rehearsal of motor tasks, from doing back flips off diving boards and shooting three-pointers to presenting speeches before audiences, moving across a stage gracefully, imagining our gestures flawless.

Cerebral Cortex (Cerebrum)

Climbing upward and around, we meet the amazing *cortex.* Unraveling a nylon shower sponge and laying it flat helps to illustrate that the gray matter of the cortex that covers the grapefruit-sized (Sousa, 2006b) mass is actually two square feet! Weave through its tenth-of-an-inch depth, its thousands of miles of connective fibers, its millions of intricate neural highways connecting with white matter to appreciate how the brain processes complex functions like thinking, planning, critical thinking, and controlling our emotion (Sylwester, 2007).

Corpus Callosum

The gray and white matter of what is most often known as the *cerebrum* is made up of two hemispheres connected by the *corpus callosum*, millions of nerve fibers that bridge the two hemispheres in their unique crossover

Figure 1.2   Selected Interior Brain Systems

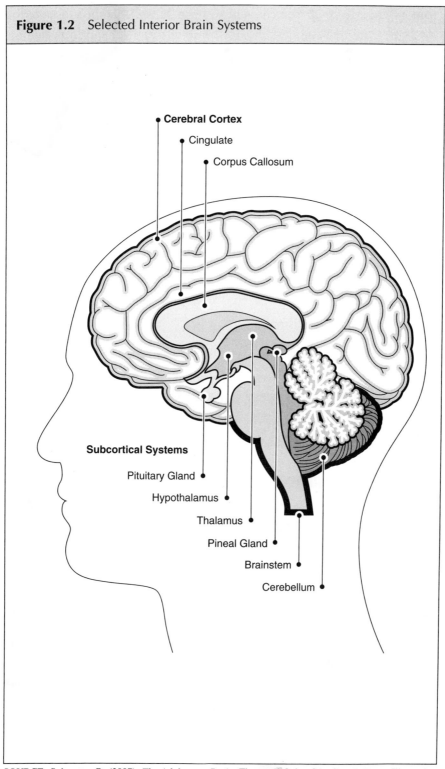

SOURCE: Sylwester, R. (2007). *The Adolescent Brain.* Thousand Oaks, CA: Corwin Press. Illustration by Peter Sylwester.

communication system. You can demonstrate for students the crossover of nerves from the right side of the body to left hemisphere and from the left side of the body to right hemisphere using a simple arm reach. Reaching your right arm across to the left side of the body is an action controlled by the *left*, not right hemisphere. Reaching your left arm across to the right side of the body is an action controlled by the *right*, not left hemisphere.

Cerebral Lobes

We observe that the wrinkles and folds of the two hemispheres appear divided into four segments or *lobes* (see Figure 1.3)—the *frontal, parietal, occipital,* and *temporal* lobes—that primarily process the following:

- *frontal lobes*: decision making, higher order thinking, problem solving, working memory

- *parietal lobes*: space and location relationships

- *occipital lobes*: vision

- *temporal lobes*: hearing, recognition of faces and objects, memory

We will develop more effective classroom management strategies if we remember the frontal lobes do not fully develop until adulthood. Sometime our students act out because they have little choice; their ability to reason and control themselves is still forming.

Amygdala and Hippocampus

Among the structures to be discovered deep inside the temporal lobe as we traverse a hemisphere of the cerebrum's white matter are two structures particularly relevant to learning. The almond-shaped *amygdala* signals our *fight-or-flight* response to environments deemed unsafe or threatening. When students feel unsafe or threatened, they cannot help but attend to self-preservation rather than cerebral processes. Brain research most assuredly suggests that the human brain is an emotional brain: to the extent that we attend to the brain's emotional needs, we will harness all else, including authentic learning.

The importance of a threat-free classroom cannot be overemphasized. But what is threat, exactly, and how does it influence the brain and learning? When students feel threatened by intimidation, embarrassment, failure, lack of choice, and other dangers, their anxiety and fear, coordinated by the brain's amygdala, trigger the production of cortisol and epinephrine, stress hormones that put the body in a fight-or-flight survival mode. Unfortunately,

Figure 1.3 Selected Interior Brain Systems

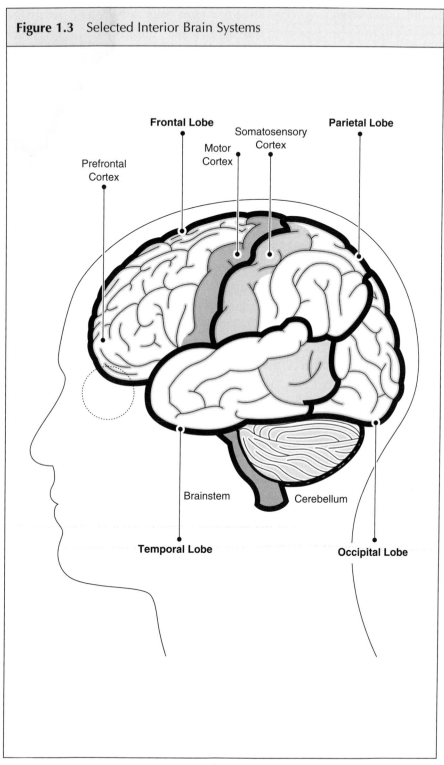

SOURCE: Sylwester, R. (2007). *The Adolescent Brain.* Thousand Oaks, CA: Corwin Press. Illustration by Peter Sylwester.

learning and other cognitive functions must take a back seat when the brain's priority is to cope with real or perceived danger.

On the other hand, what happens when learners feel safe, supported, and trusted? The brain can relax and learning can soar. Teachers who consistently provide respectful encouragement, feedback, and choice create classrooms where learning naturally happens. For example, the brain's response to choice usually includes an increased production of serotonin, dopamine, and noradrenaline. These chemicals are known to enhance a sense of well-being and motivation. Choice, therefore, may actually "feed the brain."

Students who feel safe and respected are more likely to accept challenges and sustain the motivation necessary to learn. Teachers who refrain from demanding immediate responses to their questions reduce their students' anxiety and allow them to engage in the kind of critical thinking necessary for meaningful learning to occur. Feedback that is prompt, supportive, and specific provides learners with a vital barometer by which to measure their strengths, understand and correct their weaknesses, and progress toward mastery.

Understanding that not all stress is bad is important. In fact, when we are underaroused and lack the stimulation to perform optimally, boredom can set in. Assignment deadlines, accountability pressures, and delays are just some of the stressors that are part of learners' daily lives and that, in moderate amounts, can help drive learning and achievement.

Attached to the amygdala is the seahorse-shaped *hippocampus*, essential to memory consolidation. Stress interferes with hippocampus processes involved in memory making (Sprenger, 2007), so ensuring a safe and caring environment is well advised. We may want to share with our students that our awareness of the proximity of the flight-or-fight structure of the amygdala to the memory-making structure of the hippocampus helps us appreciate the importance of creating and sustaining safe and positive environments that help make their learning experiences indeed *memorable*.

The Neuron

Our journey is not complete until we have explored the cellular structure that is the essential element of the brain: the *neuron* (see Figure 1.4). The neurons of the brain, 100 billion of them, are designed to move information. Visual, auditory, problem-solving, emotional, any information at all, is moved in a manner that may be compared to information moved through the thousands of wires, cables, and computer chips that electrically receive and send information into our homes where we experience everything from telephone conversations to virtual reality television shows.

Figure 1.4 A Functional Model of Two Related Neurons

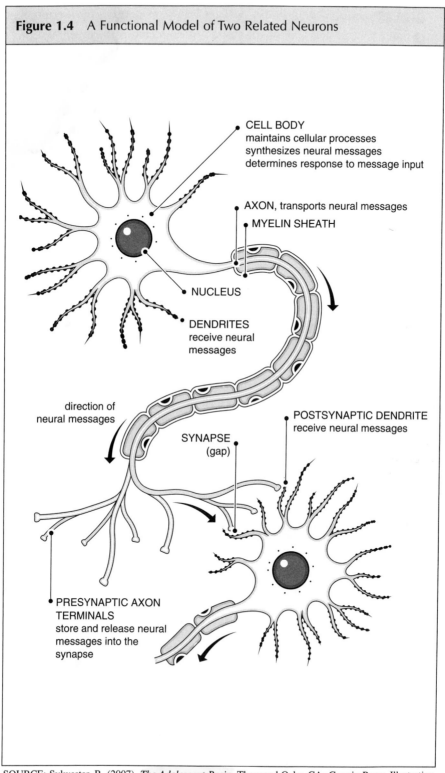

CELL BODY
maintains cellular processes
synthesizes neural messages
determines response to message input

AXON, transports neural messages
MYELIN SHEATH

NUCLEUS

DENDRITES
receive neural
messages

direction of
neural messages

SYNAPSE
(gap)

POSTSYNAPTIC DENDRITE
receive neural messages

PRESYNAPTIC AXON
TERMINALS
store and release neural
messages into the
synapse

SOURCE: Sylwester, R. (2007). *The Adolescent Brain*. Thousand Oaks, CA: Corwin Press. Illustration by Peter Sylwester.

Each neuron is its own information processor, its own little computer chip. Each neuron has tens of thousands of connections to other neurons! Like any computerized system, the brain's approximately 100 billion neurons rely on their unique and intricate hardware system to perform input and output processes. The neuron's primary mechanisms are *dendrites*, *axons*, and *synapses*. *Dendrites*, the input hardware of the neuron, are lacelike branches that receive information from other neurons. The *axon*, the output hardware of each neuron, is an armlike structure that sends information to the tens of thousands of dendrite branches of *each* neuron waiting to receive information. *Synapses* are miniscule gaps that serve as the brain's processing conduits. Learning happens when electrical and chemical (*neurotransmitter*) activities enable the axon of one neuron to *transmit* information to the receiving dendrites of another. Caskey and Ruben (2003) suggested that evidence of synaptic pruning occurring during adolescence helps to explain the adage "Use it or lose it." Connections that are reinforced through repetition are strengthened, whereas those connections that are not reinforced are pruned away. Daily practice of correct skills will help students make the connections necessary to identify errors when they present themselves in their writing or on high-stakes tests (see Chapter 2).

The 100 billion neural axons electrochemically communicating with the ten thousand dendrite branches of *each* of the billion neurons makes for one incomprehensible number of potential synaptic events and one mighty powerful supercomputer that is the brain. Imagine how excited students will become when they know the potential power of their brains and the importance of the adage "Use it or lose it"!

CELEBRATING THE LEARNING BRAIN

As technology advances, brain researchers and science have been able to use newer and more sophisticated techniques and methods to monitor brain activity. They have discovered there are few absolutes regarding brain components and their functionality (Jensen, 2007). We do know that the brain's plasticity enables it to change, to accommodate the myriad of events, accidents, trauma, and disappointments each person experiences. We should celebrate the brain's resilience and malleability as it pursues its quest to learn. One study (Draganski et al., 2004) that illustrated the plasticity of the learning brain used MRI images of the brains of student jugglers. Images showed an increased density in the part of the brain (i.e., occipital lobes) responsible for vision as students learned how to juggle three balls. However, when the students stopped practicing, they lost their juggling skills and the

MORE ABOUT THE BRAIN

Often the only familiarity students have with the brain and scientists is what they know from movies and tales about Dr. Frankenstein. When they ask questions (and they will) about how scientists really learn about the brain and its functionality, encourage them to do research on the brain. Invite them to search the Internet to learn more about the incredible technology science uses. Provide them with a list of keyword suggestions such as *magnetic resonance imaging* (MRI), *functional magnetic resonance imaging* (FMRI), and *positron emission tomography* (PET). Be sure to offer several Web resources that will help them learn more about the amazing brain. Here are a few:

Brain Connections at http://www.brainconnections.com

The Dana Foundation's Brain Kids at http://www.dana.org/resources/brainykids/

National Institute of Environmental Health Services Kids' Pages at http://kids.niehs.nih.gov/home.htm

brain density that had occurred as well, the brain region returning to its original density, graphically demonstrating "Use it or lose it."

Another study (Immordino-Yang, 2005) demonstrating plasticity involved two subjects, both boys, both successful in school, who had brain hemispheres removed due to seizures—one boy, the right hemisphere at age three; the other, the left hemisphere at age eleven. Findings suggested their brains capitalized on the strengths of their existing hemispheres and adapted them to fulfill the processing roles of their missing hemispheres.

Sharing such stories about the brain with our students helps them understand how their brains are truly supercomputers that can adjust and compensate and have the capacity to override incredible obstacles.

TWENTY-FIRST CENTURY BRAIN-COMPATIBLE TEACHERS

If we hope to become or remain brain-compatible teachers, we need a resource like the brain-compatible framework for student achievement because it relies on research related to the single most important issue driving NCLB legislation and state and district decisions: high-stakes test *results*.

The framework can arm us with the resources to keep our classroom practices and core values intact rather than give them up for packaged promises of higher test scores. Even better, we can take comfort in the knowledge that even while we rely on research related to higher test scores, we know we are really defending what we truly believe in: brain-compatible teaching.

Research on the psychological syndrome of burnout in the NCLB teaching environment led me to discover significant numbers of teachers are dissatisfied with being forced to implement programs they do not believe in (e.g., Abrams, Pedulla, & Madaus, 2003; Clarke et al., 2003; Moon, Callahan, & Tomlinson, 2003). It becomes critically important, therefore, that teachers find ways to arm themselves with research related to student achievement so they can better defend the brain-friendly decisions they make in their classrooms. Unless teachers can defend their brain-compatible teaching practices with research findings that illustrate the compatibility of their practices with student achievement, they will be unable to question and challenge school and district directives to replace best practice with test practice. Administrators, likewise, understanding that brain-compatible classroom principles are compatible with research-based propositions (NBPTS, 2007) and features that foster student achievement (Langer, 2000, 2004), may better defend leadership decisions that work to keep safe their students' brains as well as their test scores.

TWENTY-FIRST CENTURY HIGH-STAKES-TESTED STUDENTS

How very different today's students are when compared to their pre-NCLB counterparts focused on in the first edition of this book. The pressure of high-stakes mandates has piled high their desks with standardized tests in reading, mathematics, writing, science, and more. Add the testing pressure to the plate of pressures our students already endure: pressures to have the right friends, the perfect body, complexion, clothes and, worse, pressures to survive poverty, neglect, abuse, and illegal entry status. What of our English language learners who struggle with communication barriers? State laws often mandate districts to mainstream English language learners into regular classes before they have mastered even their own languages, let alone English.

Beyond what school records report, how little we know about the outside lives and inner thoughts of our high-stakes-tested students. They speak in a cell phone language that connects them with friends, family, and music. They write in a text message code whose abbreviations and syntax confound the most astute language arts teachers (especially those who remember phones with dials, not buttons). Cellular-phone language has made teaching effective oral and written communication skills more challenging than ever before and may even alter our notion of effective communication.

CAN YOU HEAR ME NOW?

Educators of all types, from teachers to board members, but especially writing teachers and coaches, must remain motivated in their desire to help students of all ages, colors, and creeds know the power of high literacy skills.

I hope the following chapters help you discover how brain-friendly approaches to learning harmonize with core propositions related to accomplished teaching and the six features of effective instruction that foster high literacy *and* high performance on tests. Collectively, each chapter's commentary, stories, examples, and reflections provide teachers a comprehensive road map. If used, the map will help teachers design defensible plans for their brain-compatible classrooms, plans that help ensure students will not only survive but thrive within their high-stakes-testing classrooms.

As stated in the preface, the following chapters are organized around six research-based features of effective instruction that fostered achievement among students in schools with poor and diverse student populations (Langer, 2000, 2004).

SIX FEATURES OF EFFECTIVE INSTRUCTION

1. Successful teachers make connections across instruction, curriculum, and life.

2. Students learn skills in multiple lesson types.

3. Successful teachers integrate test preparation into instruction.

4. Students learn strategies for doing the work.

5. Students are expected to be generative thinkers.

6. Classrooms foster cognitive collaboration.

The setting of the study (Langer, 2000) is significant because students in such settings are the very students identified by NCLB in its drive to close the achievement gap. *Beating the odds*, part of the study's title, is exactly what the teachers in the study did.

The next six chapters describe for you the features of effective instruction that emerged as patterns in schools where teachers were beating the odds and helping students not only succeed on high-stakes tests but also learn. I hope exploration of the six features within the brain-compatible framework for student achievement will help you discover how you might defend your best practice against test practice.

QUESTIONS FOR REFLECTION

1. How well does your classroom reflect a safe, caring, and supportive environment for all students?

2. To what extent do your learners feel their unique qualities and learning styles are respected and encouraged?

3. In what ways and how often do you facilitate interesting, novel, and challenging activities in your classroom?

4. In what ways and how often do you tap into learners' existing memories when presenting new topics or engaging students in learning activities?

2 Making Connections Across Instruction, Curriculum, and Life

One cannot think critically about trivial or purposeless matters.
                                            —Frank Smith, *To Think*

Feature 1

**Successful teachers make connections
across instruction, curriculum, and life.**

As mentioned in the introduction, research findings from the National Research Center on English Language & Achievement identified six features that teachers in higher performing schools exhibited (Langer, 2000, 2004). Among those features was Feature 1: *Successful teachers make connections across instruction, curriculum, and life.* This chapter describes the characteristics of the feature and explores how those characteristics complement specific brain-compatible principles and NBPTS core propositions related to accomplished teaching.

Although it is not necessary that all the components of the framework complement one another in every situation, Feature 1 does connect, in fact, with all the propositions and principles. For practical purposes we will limit our look inside the brain-compatible framework for student achievement and see how the feature related to teachers who make connections harmonizes with

- Brain-Compatible Principles 1–4: safety, respect, novelty, and memory;
- Core Propositions 2–4: knowledge of subjects and how to teach those subjects; responsibility for managing and monitoring student learning; systematic thinking about best practice and learning from experience (see Figure 2.1).

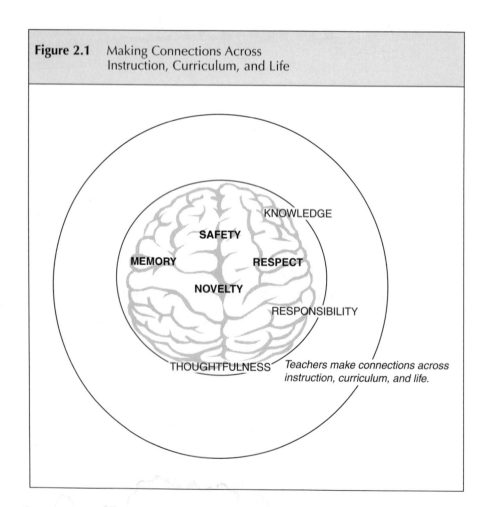

Figure 2.1   Making Connections Across Instruction, Curriculum, and Life

KNOWLEDGE

SAFETY

MEMORY

RESPECT

NOVELTY

RESPONSIBILITY

THOUGHTFULNESS   *Teachers make connections across instruction, curriculum, and life.*

Remember, by associating the brain-compatible classroom principles you believe in with research on student achievement, you may be better able to distance yourself from teach-to-the-test practices and strengthen your ability to advocate on behalf of your students and the needs of their learning brains.

CHARACTERISTICS OF FEATURE 1

Research findings suggest that language arts teachers who make connections between and across instruction, curriculum, and students' lives groom students who perform well on high-stakes tests. Effective teachers explicitly made connections "among concepts and experiences within lessons, across lessons, classes and even grades, and between in-school and out-of-school knowledge and experiences" (Langer, 2000, pp. 29–30).

By contrast, typical teachers, those whose students did not perform well on high-stakes tests, failed to make connections; even when connections were obvious, they were left implicit. Leaving unmentioned the similarities between a minor and major character *within* a (reading) lesson would illustrate this instructional faux pas.

Typical teachers seemed to view their curricula as knowledge and skills to be packaged in discrete lessons presented one after another with start points and end points. It should come as no surprise that effective teachers—the teachers who made connections across instruction, curriculum, and life—were those who, in fostering high literacy, fostered higher performing students on test days. Importantly, all of the excellent teachers in typical schools, that is, those teachers whose students beat the odds and performed higher than other students within the school, used all three approaches to making connections. The findings illustrate how one teacher can make the difference.

Have you ever had an unexpected surprise occur during a lesson? A visitor, a fire drill, a piece of technology failing you? Rather than give up on your lesson, did you somehow manage to weave the unexpected surprise into your lesson? If you did, you were modeling a characteristic of the effective teachers identified in Feature 1.

Have you ever invited students to discuss or write about a character or theme from one book or story in relation to a new character or theme? If so, you were modeling a characteristic of the effective teachers identified in Feature 1.

Rather than view a school field trip as a lost instructional day, have you ever capitalized on it, connecting the out-of-school experience with a writing form you were working on? Again, if so, you were modeling a characteristic of the effective teachers identified in Feature 1.

> ## JOHN'S STORY
>
> John was a quiet loner who spoke only when called upon. When he was in my seventh-grade class, he read aloud adequately but never volunteered. He minimally interacted with fellow students during group activities and did so only with the patient encouragement of his classmates. John seldom spoke to his peers and when he did, he mumbled. When I tried to converse with John (and it did not matter how softly I spoke), John tensed up, pressing his arms into his torso inward and spoke with much hesitation. In an effort to ease his dis-ease, I used neutral tones and succinct directives when speaking to him.

REFLECTING ON THE BRAIN-COMPATIBLE FRAMEWORK AND FEATURE 1

Research (Cavalluzzo, 2004; Goldhaber, 2004; Smith, 2005; Vandevoort, 2004) attesting to the higher student achievement record of NBCTs does not surprise me. An NBCT for ten years, I have facilitated numerous candidacy workshops and recently successfully renewed my certification for another ten. My deep knowledge of the process recognizes that the core propositions are all about making connections. Through a rigorous assessment process, NBCTs demonstrate we know the curricula and standards for which we are responsible; we think deeply about the organization and planning necessary to connect our subject standards and curricular objectives to the students we teach in meaningful ways; and we reflect on our teaching practice to help our students learn in meaningful ways. The actions of the effective teachers described by Feature 1, capitalizing on out-of-school experiences and making connections across and within lessons, are similar to the actions of NBCTs.

Brain-friendly teachers who successfully deliver instruction in novel and engaging ways are reminiscent of NBCTs when you consider the planning involved in developing lessons and activities that engage students and harness existing memories to influence genuine learning opportunities.

THE BRAIN-COMPATIBLE FRAMEWORK WITH FEATURE 1 IN ACTION

For teachers to make connections across instruction, curriculum, and life, they must be willing to plan, plan, plan. To make connections on a daily basis involves learning our standards, our subject content, and the curricular objectives we are expected to satisfy, and learning about our students yearly or quarterly. The more planning that takes place behind the scenes, the more readily we will be able to make connections with what goes on in and across the classrooms, grades, and lives of our students. Part of that planning involves learning about the students we will care for so that we know how to teach them in ways that are meaningful to them and respectful of them.

LEARNING ABOUT OUR STUDENTS

In *Celebration of Neurons*, Dr. Robert Sylwester (1995) explains that the brain learns best if the environment is safe and caring. How much learning would happen if every learner in every classroom felt safe and cared for? As teachers it is crucial that we treat all of our students joyously and with great care, not just our low-maintenance students who are so easy to care for, but our melancholy and challenging students, particularly those whom we are tempted to view as troublemakers, failures with too many problems, too many needs.

When we think about caring for our students, we must realize caring does not mean the same thing as babying them. Care and discipline complement each other because teachers who discipline fairly, consistently, and dispassionately reflect genuine care of students who, consequently, are more likely to accept consequences and take responsibility for their actions.

Discipline can and must be a demonstration of care. Children are wise. They discern fair from unfair discipline. They need people in their lives who can help them learn how to respect and follow acceptable parameters. They need to be held accountable by adults who mete out consequences for misbehavior or misdeeds without injuring their self-concept. Weissbourd (2003) calls such teachers *moral* teachers,

> those who groom moral students not simply by being good role models—important as that is—but also by what they bring to their relationships with students day to day: their ability to appreciate students' perspectives and to disentangle them from their own, their ability to admit and learn from moral error, their moral energy and idealism, their generosity, and their ability to help students develop moral thinking without shying away from their own moral authority. (pp. 6–7)

Genuinely committing ourselves to the welfare of all our children is essential if we are to help all our high-stakes-tested students. No amount of teaching content will help children learn unless all existing and future educators learn how vital it is to create brain-compatible, safe, nurturing environments where all students feel wanted, even if only for a short time in their day. Only then will students see their schools as safe places where they can thrive academically and socially.

Multiple Intelligences

One way to learn about our students is by considering the *multiple intelligences*, a term first coined by Howard Gardner (1985), a professor of graduate education at Harvard University. Gardner, while examining the nature of intelligence and alternate ways of thinking about it, discovered that intelligence is largely defined by one's culture and that the array of human learning styles and intelligences can be broken into categories described briefly as follows:

- *Verbal/linguistic (V/L)*: reading, vocabulary, and verbal communication skills such as storytelling, humor, jokes, and verbal debate
- *Visual/spatial (V/S)*: guided imagery, drawing, painting, mind mapping, pictures, and other visual aids
- *Bodily/kinesthetic (B/K)*: movement and hands-on activities such as experiments, dance, gestures, role playing, field trips, games, and sports
- *Logical/mathematical (L/M)*: calculations, abstract symbols, number sequences, codes, problem solving, and patterns
- *Musical/rhythmic (M/R)*: song, rhythmic patterns, music, vocal tones, and environmental sounds
- *Interpersonal/social (I/S)*: collaboration, interaction, and communication
- *Intrapersonal (I)*: reflection, introspection, strategic thinking, focused concentration, and working independently
- *Naturalist (N)*: sensitivity to environment, ability to use sensory input from nature to survive

WRITING AND THE MULTIPLE INTELLIGENCES

With the stroke of a pencil, pen, or keystroke, writers express real or imagined sensory experiences. Writing is a dynamic manifestation of creative and critical thinking skills. Both a sensorimotor and cognitive process, writing serves all of Howard Gardner's multiple intelligences, not just verbal/linguistic. To illustrate, writing serves the music intelligence when maestros share their genius through written composition. Writing serves bodily/kinesthetic intelligence when coaches write strategic plays their athletes execute. Writing serves logical/mathematical intelligence when scientists write proofs to theories; visual/spatial when architects write to defend how their designs will successfully interface with existing structures; and interpersonal, intrapersonal, and naturalist intelligences when individuals become therapists, speechwriters, novelists, philosophers, and environmentalists.

To which of the multiple intelligences do you relate? Do you prefer working alone or with others? Do you prefer to learn about a topic via reading or hands-on activities? Would music enhance or diminish your learning experience? Reflecting on the multiple intelligences and respecting the legitimacy of learning style preferences can help us plan more diverse and appealing activities to better meet the needs of our diverse learners.

BRAIN SURVEYS

To learn about my students and their learning preferences, I start from the first day by using the *Getting to Know You* survey that follows.

GETTING TO KNOW YOU

Name_____

Please complete the following statements.

I'm the student who _____

_____

My birth name is _____

My nickname is _____

Circle only the items you feel describe you <u>most accurately</u>:

1. I like to draw.
2. I like to whistle or hum.
3. I like to solve problems and puzzles.
4. I love to dance.
5. I like organizing outdoor activities.
6. I enjoy thinking about ideas that are on my mind.
7. I enjoy reading.
8. I enjoy talking with friends.
9. I love to hang out with friends.
10. I like to sing.
11. I enjoy figuring out codes.
12. I prefer to work on projects by myself.
13. I enjoy the game of chess.
14. I enjoy writing stories and poems.

(Continued)

(Continued)

15. I enjoy sculpting clay or creating collages.
16. I love hiking and camping.
17. I often use hand and body gestures while I speak. 18. I can listen to music for hours.
19. I wish I could play a musical instrument or I'm glad I play an instrument.
20. I like math or anything to do with numbers.
21. I like to write stories.
22. I like studying the stars.
23. I like to design new things.
24. I can picture things in my mind easily.
25. I enjoy working on one thing for a long period of time.
26. To relax I would rather go for a walk than sit.
27. I prefer to work in teams or groups.
28. I have a good understanding of myself.
29. I sense when my friends are upset and often know how to help them.
30. I enjoy working and playing with animals.
31. I'm good at oral debates.
32. I like to play sports.

Add anything else you would like me to know about you as a learner—or about you!

_____

_____

_____

_____

_____

Thank you!

I'm the Student Who . . .

When students tell me about themselves by completing the part in the survey *I'm the student who* . . . , they provide me with unique characteristics or experiences with which I can connect their names. For example, "I'm the one who broke my arm on the trampoline, plays the violin, has four dogs." One student I have never forgotten wrote, "I'm the one who stuffed my sister's teddy bear down the toilet when I was 4 years old." I use these personal comments as biographical *mnemonics*; they help me learn all my students' names as well as giving me a concrete starting point for getting to know them better.

By the time I am ready to establish my seating charts (see Chapter 7), the third day of school, I have already completed a lot of work! I've read, analyzed, and ultimately organized students into six or seven groups based on survey information. I write my students' biographical mnemonic near their names. The memory tool has consistently helped me to know everyone's names by the end of week one.

Survey information also helps me place within each group at least one student self-identified as verbal/linguistic. These students often become leaders within their writing groups, modeling the art of writing as they increase their neural connections and pathways of understanding. Learning from survey responses that I do not have at least five self-identified verbal/ linguistic students in a class or classes alerts me to the possibility that these classes of students may need more instructional time as well as different types of instruction. (By the way, I also make sure to disperse my interpersonal students to avoid excess chatter!)

Coloring Brains

Once students have completed the survey, have them use the *Color Your Brain* directions (see Figure 2.2) and key (see Figure 2.3) to tally their scores and color their brains. (For very young students, you may want to complete this task yourself.) Letter codes used in the key (i.e., V/L, L/M) represent each of the intelligences introduced by Howard Gardner. Writing appropriate letter codes near student names on my seating charts help remind me of each student's answers. As your students learn about Gardner's multiple intelligences, you may want to discuss visual, auditory, and kinesthetic learning-style preferences. (The more students know about how their brains learn, the better!)

Color Your Brain Directions to Share With Students

- Using the *Color Your Brain* key, revisit the numbers you circled.
- For each intelligence category, count the circles you have for each set of numbers shown. Notice each of the intelligences has a letter code.

○ For example, for verbal/linguistic, V/L, you will look at 7, 14, 21, and 31 and total those statements you circled. If you circled 7, 14, and 21, your V/L score would be 3.

● Count the circled numbers for each of the intelligences and write each total on the appropriate line.

○ For example, if your V/L score is 3, write 3 on the TOTAL line near V/L.

Figure 2.2 *Color Your Brain* Directions

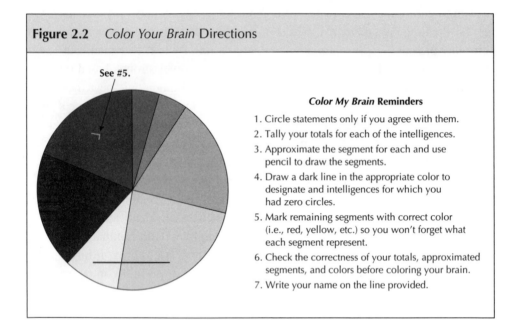

See #5.

***Color My Brain* Reminders**

1. Circle statements only if you agree with them.
2. Tally your totals for each of the intelligences.
3. Approximate the segment for each and use pencil to draw the segments.
4. Draw a dark line in the appropriate color to designate and intelligences for which you had zero circles.
5. Mark remaining segments with correct color (i.e., red, yellow, etc.) so you won't forget what each segment represent.
6. Check the correctness of your totals, approximated segments, and colors before coloring your brain.
7. Write your name on the line provided.

Segments on the oval (representing the brain) help students approximate how much space to allow for each of their intelligences based on survey results. For example, students who have the same totals for several intelligences will approximate the same amount of space for those intelligences using different colors accordingly.

When students have a zero for one of the intelligences, assure them their brains are fine! After all, there are only four statements for each category, and the survey is simply a way to help students learn about the concept of multiple intelligences, reflect on their learning style preferences, and help you get to know them.

To signify the intelligence that scores zero, I invite students to draw a thick line and color it the appropriate color.

Invite students to use the color code provided and to write their names on the line indicated before they cut their brains out and post them on the wall. (Gee, I love saying that.)

Figure 2.3 *Color Your Brain*

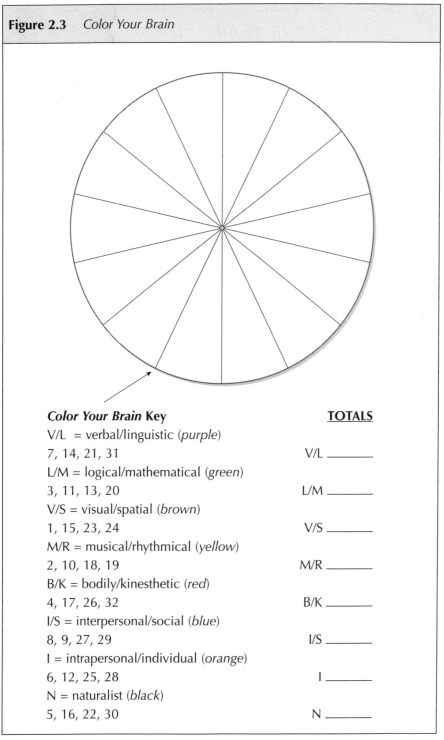

Color Your Brain Key

TOTALS

V/L = verbal/linguistic (*purple*)
7, 14, 21, 31   V/L _____

L/M = logical/mathematical (*green*)
3, 11, 13, 20   L/M _____

V/S = visual/spatial (*brown*)
1, 15, 23, 24   V/S _____

M/R = musical/rhythmical (*yellow*)
2, 10, 18, 19   M/R _____

B/K = bodily/kinesthetic (*red*)
4, 17, 26, 32   B/K _____

I/S = interpersonal/social (*blue*)
8, 9, 27, 29   I/S _____

I = intrapersonal/individual (*orange*)
6, 12, 25, 28   I _____

N = naturalist (*black*)
5, 16, 22, 30   N _____

Calling All Teachers!

Here are some variations to the basic instructions that have been already presented.

ELEMENTARY SCHOOL TEACHERS. You may need to modify the activity by

- cutting the paper brains ahead of time;
- reading the statements aloud to students, pausing after each one to check for understanding;
- bringing worksheets home to tally yourself. You can divide each student's paper brain for coloring, identifying each segment you have marked off with the appropriate crayon color.

MIDDLE AND HIGH SCHOOL TEACHERS. Invite students to create collages that display their colored brains and use photos, magazine clips, and other aids to reflect each of their self-identified intelligences.

WRITING CONNECTIONS

After learning about our students, we need to think about planning what and how we teach. And because writing is a huge part of what and how we teach—especially, but not exclusively, for language arts teachers—we really should reflect on what writing instruction means and what it means to us personally. By thinking about the writing process, we may be better prepared to make explicit connections across instruction, curriculum, and our students' lives.

WRITING: PLEASURE OR PAIN?

Writing can be a pleasant experience, the tool by which ideas and memories spill onto pages and computer screens. On the other hand, writing can be a painful experience that blocks and stalls ideas and memories, causing writers, teachers, or students to feel frustrated and insecure. We can resolve from the beginning of the school year to help students remain willing (if not motivated) writers by creating safe and supportive writing-process settings.

Writing helps the brain organize and reflect. Writing enables students to make sense of complex, multifaceted pieces of information. Journaling and other note-taking forms provide written records for review and reflection that enhance both immediate and long-term recall ability. Reflective journaling can also help the emotional brain. A two-part study on the effects of expressive writing on the working memory, for example, conducted by Klein and Boals (2001) revealed that individuals who wrote reflective narratives about negative experiences experienced a decline in dissonant, avoidance thinking related to the events. Such findings suggest that writing may provide a healthy and productive way to improve memory and deal with trauma, offering not just an important life skill but also a life-coping skill.

Planning a winning training season for young writers is not a prescriptive exercise. The key is to establish an overall instructional plan that serves as a foundation for implementing, modifying, and refining daily learning activities. If brain research scientists like Marian Diamond (Diamond & Hopson, 1998) have taught us anything, it is that no two children learn exactly alike. Thus we need to have a learning plan, in fact, a multilayered plan that provides for flexibility and accommodation. If we haven't considered the need for a *Plan B,* how will we proceed when *Plan A* fails?

If we all had the luxury of teaching dedicated, serious-minded students, each one of them voluntarily tuned in to learning, our jobs would be easy. Clearly, then, we must design writing activities that will hook fledgling writers the way published writers hook readers, from the very start.

We will hook our student writers only if we have a clear understanding of our standards and curriculum objectives and a well-developed and organized plan of when and how we will teach writing. Our success as teachers who can make connections across instruction, curriculum, and life requires planning, planning, and planning. Planning workshop environments such as those described in the first edition of my book and in Atwell's seminal work (1990) will help you get started. With or without workshop environments, we all need to learn more about writing if we want to be writing coaches as well as teachers.

WRITING ON DEMAND

If we want to be writing coaches as well as writers, we need to understand writing and the process of writing. Writing can be expressive, descriptive, narrative, expository, or persuasive. It can involve untimed *process writing*, which traditionally includes brainstorming, drafting, conferencing, revising, editing, and finalizing. Writing can also be a timed process often called *demand writing*, whereby writing is timed and specific to prompts like the prompts found on high-stakes writing tests (see Chapter 4). Writing on demand often carries more stress for young writers than they experience during process writing. Grooming students to be proficient in both types of writing requires a safe and enriched learning environment, and that happens only when teachers know their subject and know that to teach it requires thoughtful and systematic planning. If the conditions remind you of NBPTS core propositions, good for you! You are beginning to recognize the harmony among the three components of the brain-compatible framework for student achievement.

Planning

To help the brain make connections that lead to writing mastery, a strategic plan must be in place that helps to develop the strengths of young writers. The plan must attend to the challenges inherent in each type of writing. I recommend beginning the school year with more expressive types of writing, description and narration, which readily tap into existing episodic memories and sensory experiences. Within the safety of their own memories and creative thoughts, students may write more willingly.

Piaget (2008) suggested that when introducing experiences that initially produce some struggle, students need tools to resolve their cognitive difficulties. Applying the notion to writing, we might help students by providing them with examples of topics from which to choose and help them remember episodes from their past by inviting students to recall experiences that made them happy, sad, embarrassed, and the like. Encourage them during the drafting stages. Use student writing to provide proof that students do indeed have something to write about. Empower and instill students with confidence to move on to the more challenging forms of writing, exposition and persuasion, which require higher order thinking skills. Provide them with writing activities that are both challenging and engaging. Ask them to argue a controversial topic using a letter-to-the-editor format. Invite them to write cover letters that persuade employers to hire them. Allow them to express their feelings through poetry.

No matter what students are writing, allow them to compose freely. Being unimpeded by analytical cognitive processes that monitor mechanical skills, for example, frees students' cognitive thought processes to more readily tap into memories, ideas, and opinions. Researcher and educator Frank Smith (1986) described a study conducted by two leaders in writing pedagogy, Donald Graves and Lucy Calkins, whereby third-grade students were encouraged to write using their own punctuation. By year's end the children who had no formal training demonstrated a greater command of punctuation and its function than those who had had typical skill and drill training. (See Chapter 3.)

Modeling

Social cognitive theorist Albert Bandura (1994) has emphasized that learners are motivated to learn when their own levels of competence and self-efficacy are high and when they perceive activities as meaningful. There is no better way to promote the self-efficacy levels of students and to make the writing process more meaningful than for teachers to act as coaches who take part in that process, sharing their abilities with their fledgling writers.

Writing becomes more meaningful and less threatening for students when they identify their teachers as fellow writers who brainstorm topics, compose drafts, discuss experiences, share frustrations, and ultimately produce final products. Model for students how real writers write—and rewrite. Enhance writing environments with frequent feedback, peer and teacher interaction, and stimulating and meaningful writing opportunities. Make sure that peer model samples are also plentiful to help students of all age levels and abilities learn from others in their own age groups.

STRATEGIC FLEXIBILITY

An understanding of Piaget's stages of cognitive theory of development enables writing coaches to understand that moving from young child to adolescent stages means moving from concrete to more imaginative and abstract thought. You can help the youngest groups of writers by scribing for them as they excitedly recount memories faster than they themselves can write them down. Prepare handouts containing a series of *I remember* blanks to help youngsters identify memories they might write about (e.g., a time they were frightened, happy, sad, lonely, angry, excited). Be receptive to all memories, happy, sad, or serious. I once conducted a writing workshop at an inner-city school. After inviting the third graders to think about a time they were happy, sad, or excited, a few students shared memories (corroborated by the teacher) of drive-by bullets shattering their living room windows and parents whom they seldom saw because they worked day and night shifts. Current understanding about the brain's ability to self-repair (Ross, 2006) punctuates the importance of providing students opportunities to write about their sad or traumatic as well as (and maybe even more so than) their happier experiences.

Cognitive Freedom

Provide writers the cognitive freedom to demonstrate ability in their own way. If students struggle with expository essays, help them make connections to other writing products (and consequently their audiences) such as newspaper articles or letters. Provide writers flexibility and opportunity to demonstrate *their* ability, guiding them beyond what Piaget called *disequilibrium*, cognitive conflict, to self-confidence and discovery. Their tools: reassurance, encouragement, and empowerment.

Teaching and Coaching

To transform ourselves into writing coaches, it's helpful to rethink how we use our plan books. I use my mine like a journal. I jot down observations about what worked and what didn't. Doing so improves my creativity, effectiveness, and long-term planning. By writing about and reflecting on our teaching practices, we dialogue with our brains, firing neural pathways, connecting ideas about failed plans and winning plans, how we might produce better, new and improved plans that help us to become not just good writing instructors, but effective and accomplished teachers who serve more as writing coaches.

Our thoughtfully planned lessons and units of instruction can help our students become better writers. Allegations that planning stifles spontaneity and creativity are preposterous. Can you imagine Microsoft or General Electric allowing employees to do whatever they want on the job? Of course not! Functional environments, be they in education or business, tend to maintain clear job descriptions and guidelines with enough flexibility to accommodate individual expression and personal choice. This balance is the hallmark that unites authentically successful companies and classrooms. Rather than preventing teachable moments, sound planning multiplies them!

Planning the plan and playing the plan make the hard work involved worthwhile. Playing the plan well has the potential to distinguish us as effective, accomplished, and brain-compatible teachers who recognize and seize opportunities to make connections across instruction, curriculum, and life.

SEVEN STAGES OF BRAIN-FRIENDLY WRITING INSTRUCTION

Now that we have made some important connections to writing and what it means to be a writing teacher and coach, we should consider another important aspect of writing I refer to as the *seven stages of brain-friendly writing instruction*. I rely on John, the quiet boy we met earlier in this chapter, to

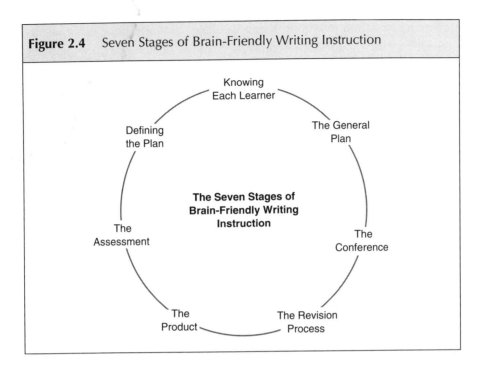

Figure 2.4 Seven Stages of Brain-Friendly Writing Instruction

help me describe the seven stages. Figure 2.4 depicts the symbiotic relationship of the seven stages.

Please remember. The stages of writing, like the process, are not prescriptive. Once the first writing assignment is complete, defining the plan for each student becomes the start point for future writings.

Stage 1: Knowing Each Learner

On the first day of school, John indicated in his brain survey (more about the survey later on in this chapter) that he enjoyed music, which would later become the topic of his first writing assignment. He also revealed a vital bit of personal information when he completed the sentence, "I'm the one who . . . has seven sisters." These facets of John's life—his love of music and his crowded home environment—helped me determine what cues might motivate him to write (connecting John to his home life).

Stage 2: The General Plan

To prepare John and his classmates for the new quarter, I had the class complete three brief writing exercises that focused on using our five senses to evoke powerful images in our writing. Students sometimes reduce the task of descriptive writing to the mundane. "I could smell the sweet candy. I could taste it, too." To maximize learner success, I challenged them to imagine a camera in their mind's eye and to keep that camera rolling as a technique for producing authentic sensory images (see Chapter 6). For their first homework assignment, students were asked to watch television, which of course immediately sparked their interest. This was followed up with a request to choose a favorite television commercial and write down what images it conveyed. The next day students volunteered to share their images with the class, challenging each other to guess what commercial they were describing. By the end of the exercise, everyone agreed that words and, ultimately, writers produce the images.

Introducing description strategies early in the year and reinforcing them throughout helps learners integrate sensory images into all of their writing pieces. For feedback and follow-up, learners compare and evaluate their images using writing rubrics for *word choice* and *sentence fluency* to guide them (see Chapter 5). By this time students understand the value and power of description within their writing pieces and are ready to compose their own prose or poetry.

Stage 3: The Conference

During conferencing I meet with students to discuss their accomplishments and challenge areas. It's always important to guard fragile egos before offering ideas or suggesting revisions, but experience had taught me that with John it was especially important. On the first day of school, when I invited students to tell me about themselves in their *I'm the one who* activity, John also wrote of an incident in which he and a friend had egged a child and then laughed and teased the child's angry mother. When I tried to talk with John about the incident (thinking he might he kidding), I discovered his difficulty (both physical and emotional) with social interaction. A call home, one of many, to learn more about John revealed a rather impatient attitude on his mother's part towards her "difficult" son. My informal conference and call provided further insight into John and his home environment, information that helped me during subsequent conferences.

Stage 4: The Revision Process

I encouraged John to view his first attempt at writing the poem "Concerts" as a draft that would benefit from the revision process. I complimented the format of his poem, interpreting what I saw as his application of my workshop lesson on *line break* in poetry. I also asked John if his alliterative initiation of many lines beginning with *s* words was intentional. He shrugged uncomfortably. I lightheartedly told him he was being modest, hoping to encourage him to complete the piece. I invited him to use my classroom computer. He accepted.

Stage 5: The Finished Product

In the rough draft of his poem, John incorporated three of the five senses effectively. This was more than acceptable because I had cautioned students not to use trite or forced images merely for the sake of including all five senses. On his first draft, John crossed out the negative, albeit dramatic,

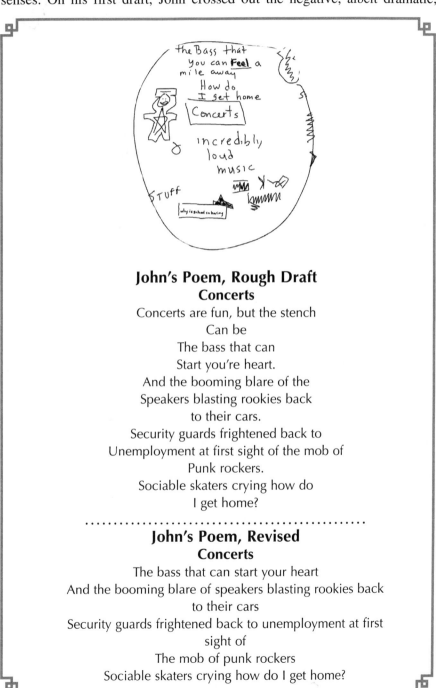

John's Poem, Rough Draft
Concerts
Concerts are fun, but the stench
Can be
The bass that can
Start you're heart.
And the booming blare of the
Speakers blasting rookies back
to their cars.
Security guards frightened back to
Unemployment at first sight of the mob of
Punk rockers.
Sociable skaters crying how do
I get home?

. . . .

John's Poem, Revised
Concerts
The bass that can start your heart
And the booming blare of speakers blasting rookies back
to their cars
Security guards frightened back to unemployment at first
sight of
The mob of punk rockers
Sociable skaters crying how do I get home?

sensory word *stench* and the trite word *fun*, demonstrating his commendable willingness and ability to control his images while actively removing the negative or banal. John also attended to mechanical flaws, such as self-correcting the spelling of *you're* to *your*.

The defining characteristic of John's revised poem is the pervasive sense of sound. John so quiet; his images, loud and deep. His percussive bass, "the booming blare of the speakers blasting," and "sociable skaters crying" inform me that he, indeed, used his "mind's camera" as directed.

Stage 6: The Assessment

I complimented John's revisions and subtly prodded him to pursue the image he intended. I asked if he meant " start your heart pumpin'." He nodded yes but chose to retain his more dramatic interpretation, "start your heart." The prewriting brainstorm activity told of "incredibly loud music," but his draft commendably produced the "booming blare." Though he relinquished his original line break (possibly) to the preset margins of computer software, John clearly kept his eye's camera rolling, and I wrote only positive comments on his cover sheet.

Stage 7: The Refined Plan

When John completed his end-of-quarter review sheet (see Chapter 5), he was honest. He wrote that he hated to brainstorm and write rough drafts. When asked how our class could be better, he stated, "If we didn't have to write stories and we didn't have to brainstorm."

Based on his response, I suggested to John that he think out the brainstorm and draft stages in his head rather than on paper. He appreciated the respect I gave his introspective prewriting and composing processes. I almost literally held my breath and crossed my fingers as he sat thinking. By honoring his writing process and preferences, I think John came to respect both his writing and me more. He eventually discovered his writing style and voice, and I discovered that John was a good writer. Though he clearly had not enjoyed self-expressive writing, he demonstrated interest and strong proficiency in each expository and persuasive piece he wrote thereafter, sometimes using the prescribed predrafting strategies he hated. He also contributed, albeit quietly, to each oral report, skit, and debate his team produced.

It is not realistic to believe all our students are willing writers in all areas. My John was not ready or willing in some ways; yet in other ways, he was. No, he never finished his personal narrative about the egging incident that he had briefly, though boldly, shared his first day of school, and I had to encourage him every step of the way to produce his image piece on concerts. But unless we challenge our students to explore and experience each kind of writing, how else will they discover their strengths and preferences? When we respect our students, their particular areas of interest, their unique abilities and preference for different kinds of writing and writing processes, we attend to their brain needs.

Upon close examination of John's brainstorm drawing that preceded his writing of "Concerts," I noticed a question he wrote that shouted volumes. His inner self leaked out in miniscule letters encased in a box: "Why is school so boring?"

How do we satisfy the needs of our young learners while we balance curriculum requirements? I admit it is a challenge. But if we believe that each student has writing strengths that we can help him or her to develop, and if we treat each learner as an individual, we will help shape that reality for each one.

If we let students know we expect their success and encourage them to expect their own success—even if it is sometimes delayed—then our efforts are not in vain. John, like many students, is a more proficient writer today because he was given opportunities to connect his writing to his life. He was given the encouragement that brain-friendly, accomplished, and effective teachers offer the students to whom they are committed. Finally, he was given the accommodations that brain-friendly teachers routinely offer to their students so they can keep their eyes safely on the prize.

Sometimes I think about John and wonder how he is, whether he overcame his shyness, whether he walks and talks a little more easily than he did when I knew him. I hope this section about John and the seven stages helped illustrate the integrity of the brain-compatible framework for student achievement by showing how brain-friendly teachers and coaches are similar to the accomplished teachers who uphold the tenets of NBPTS core propositions and the effective teachers who make connections across instruction, curriculum, and life.

The more we recognize how very much our adherence to brain-compatible classroom principles helps define us as teachers within the brain-compatible framework for student achievement, the more we empower ourselves to defend the instructional designs we plan for our classrooms.

The next pages contain samples of how I plan my school year. Examining and organizing my curricular obligations before the year starts enables me to help my students make meaningful connections that foster achievement throughout the year. I share the samples with my students, their parents, and guardians because I believe they provide evidence of my understanding of the standards for which I am responsible and evidence of my commitment to teaching in a purposeful, meaningful way. I hope the samples provide you a sense of how to plan the plan.

Figure 2.6   Seventh-Grade Language Arts Curriculum

Language Arts instructs students to become effective communicators and culturally aware citizens by integrating the following components:

reading   writing   listening   speaking   viewing

···

WRITER'S WORKSHOP

Description   Narration   Exposition   Persuasion

Process Writing

Prewriting   Drafting   Revising
Conferencing   Editing   Presenting

Demand Writing

Timed writing tests (excludes steps of process)

Reflective "Writing to Learn" Writing

Grammar, spelling, and usage will not be graded.

Personal, critical responses to learning
experienced in all content areas

Standard 2: Concept WF1, Concepts 1–8. Standard 1: Concept 6

···

READER'S WORKSHOP

Appreciating   Comprehending   Discussing
Visualizing   Writing to Respond

Standard 1: Strand 1/Concepts 5, 6. Strand 2/Concepts 1-2

···

VOCABULARY WORKSHOP

Vocabulary   Grammar   Usage   Spelling
Roots/Prefixes/Suffixes

Standard 1: Strand 1/Concept 4

···

LISTENING AND SPEAKING

Poise   Diction   Self-expression   Manners
Speech   Oral Report   Dramatic Presentation

Standard 3: Concept 1

···

VIEWING AND PRESENTING

Oral and written responses to media, art, music, literature

Standard 4: Concept 1

Note: I include curricular standards and concepts to demonstrate my understanding of and commitment to them.

Figure 2.7   Language Arts Curricular Calendar

Quarter 1: Description/Narration

Writer's Workshop:

- Process/Mechanics/Conventions
- Personal Experience Narration

Reader's Workshop

- Selections focus *on readings* with application to specific writing products: description and narration
- Independent Reading

Viewing and Presenting Component

- Reflective, analytical responses to various works of art (e.g., writing, art, music)

Vocabulary Workshop

- Literary terminology
- Roots, prefixes, suffixes, spelling, grammar, usage and vocabulary in context of quarter's objectives

Listening and Speaking Workshop

- Listening and speaking as individuals as well as in small and large groups for a variety of purposes including, e.g., interpreting writing rubrics, literature, music, and art

Quarter 2: Narration

Writer's Workshop

- Summary
- Response to Literary Selection
- Creative Story

Reader's Workshop

- Selections focus on readings with application to specific writing products: narration
- Novel Study: *Sounder* by Armstrong
- Independent Reading

Viewing and Presenting Component

- Response and or analysis of various works of art (e.g., writing, art, music)

Vocabulary Workshop

- Literary terminology
- Spelling, grammar, usage, vocabulary, all in context of quarter's writing objectives (e.g., rising action, climax; folktale, fable, myth)

Listening and Speaking Workshop

- Listening and speaking as individuals as well as in small and large groups for a variety of purposes including, e.g., interpreting writing rubrics, literature, music, and art

(Continued)

Figure 2.7 (Continued)

Quarter 3: Oral/Written Exposition

Writer's Workshop

- Research Skills
- Expository Essay

Reader's Workshop

- Selections focus *on readings* with application to specific writing products: exposition.
- Novel Study: *The Outsiders* by Hinton
- Independent Reading

Viewing and Presenting Workshop

- Evaluation, synthesis, and presentation of information to communicate effectively

Vocabulary Workshop

- Spelling, grammar, usage, vocabulary in context of quarter's objectives (e.g., propaganda techniques terminology, adjectival/adverbial clauses)

Listening and Speaking Workshop

- Listening and speaking formally as well as informally in small and large groups: *formal reporting, interviewing, dramatic interpretation*

Quarter 4: Persuasion/Research

Writer's Workshop

- Research Skills
- Formal Communication
- Point of View Report

Reader's Workshop

- Selections focus on readings with application to specific writing products: persuasion
- Drama and Novel Study (TBA)
- Independent Reading

Viewing and Presenting Workshop

- Research-based selections that generate opinions and facilitate persuasive written and oral communications

Vocabulary Workshop

- Spelling, grammar, usage, vocabulary, all in context of quarter's writing objectives (e.g., argument, conclusion, premise, major points

Listening and Speaking Workshop

- Listening and speaking as individuals as well as in small and large groups: *formal speech, reporting, dramatic interpretation*

Figure 2.8	Overview of Purposes and Products for Writing

PURPOSES	POSSIBLE PRODUCTS
I. TO DESCRIBE. To use words that appeal to the sesne in order to reveal appearance or to convey an image, impression, or feeling	• paragraph(s) describing a real or imaginary person • or place • advertisement for an object • feature article describing a place or object • classified advertisement to sell an article • poem appealing to one or more senses • friendly letter • journal entry • personal response to literature
II. TO NARRATE. To tell an imaginative (fictional) story or to give an account of real events	• narrative of actual experience • short story • journal entry • fable, folktale, or myth • skit or script • feature article • autobiographical sketch • humorous newspaper column
III. TO EXPLAIN. (Expository writing) To make factual information clear and understandable	• directions • how to . . . • letter of invitation • business letter: ordering information; of request; of • complaint • research report • news article and headline • biographical sketch based on interview • biographical report • essay: on a process; deductive essay • character study based on a work of literature • letter of application • resumé • captions (used to label)
IV. TO PERSUADE. To change the opinion of or influence the action of a particular audience	• advertisement; commercial • contest entry • letter: to persuade; for or against an issue • book review • editorial • literary analysis • argumentative essay • review of an event of performance • formal speech

SOURCE: Overview and verbs selections are adapted and printed with permission from Edith Wagner, the language arts scholar and visionary who developed the comprehensive K–12 writing program that was implemented during her tenure at the William Floyd School District in New York. Wagner is currently Associate Professor of English at Tusculum College, TN.

VERBS ARE YOUR FRIENDS

When you plan your activities, lessons, and instructional units, please think about verbs. Ask yourself: What do I want my students to do? Why do I want them to do it? Why are these activities, lessons, assignments important? Reflecting on and then choosing appropriate verbs help you envision your lessons as they unfold and consequently help you write plans that will fulfill your curricular goals in brain-compatible ways.

Describing Verbs

What-you-want-students-to-actually-do verbs: verbs that identify student actions.

Table 2.1   Describing Verbs

access	describe	operate
adapt	design	organize
add	determine	outline
adjust	develop	participate
alter	display	perform
analyze	divide	plan
apply	estimate	plot
arrange	evaluate	prepare
assemble	examine	present
bind	exhibit	read
build	expand	record
calculate	explain	research
calibrate	find	respond
categorize	formulate	review
choose	gather	revise
cite	generate	role-play
classify	identify	select
collect	interpret	sort
compare	itemize	speak
compile	justify	specify
confer	label	spell
construct	list	state
contrast	listen	subtract
convert	locate	summarize
correct	make	teach
create	match	trace
decide	measure	utilize
debate	mix	use
define	multiply	weigh
demonstrate	name	write

How, Why, *and* What *Verbs*

Big picture verbs: verbs that explain why you and your students do what you do.

They are verbs to help identify your instructional goals, objectives, and aims.

Table 2.2	*How, Why,* and *What* Verbs		
appreciate	discuss	grasp the	realize
assess	communicate	significance of	recognize
assist	comprehend	have insight into	share
assume	coordinate	know	study
be acquainted with	consider	learn	talk about
be interested in	engage	maintain	think about
be aware of	establish	monitor	understand
believe	explore	prioritize	value

PLAN TO USE REUSABLE MAGNETIZED PLACARDS

To use your instructional time more effectively, consider the verb plan. The more you plan ways to free yourself from procedural classroom chores you find yourself doing on a regular basis, the more time you will have to instruct. Here is a time saver I devised after finally realizing I was writing the same things on the board every day.

- Cut brightly colored poster paper into strips about 12 to 15 inches long and 3 to 4 inches wide. (The length will depend on what you need to write.)
- Using large block letters and a thick marker, write the words and phrases you routinely write on the board, for example, *Copy homework, Please read today's goal.*
- Fasten these handy placards on the board regularly and refer to them regularly until learners come to read them without prompting.

If you have a magnetized board, buy a set of magnet clips to fasten the placards. Business card magnets (available practically everywhere) are an inexpensive alternative to clips. Simply tape the magnetic card to the back of the construction paper banner, leaving the magnetic side free to contact the board.

(Continued)

(Continued)

> If you don't have a magnetized board, punch a hole or two at the top of the construction paper and run a sufficient length of yarn or fishing line through the holes. Tie a loop in the line and hook it over a nail or tack.
>
> Establishing efficient routines and procedures for our students to follow helps us work smarter, not harder. By using our instructional time more efficiently, our students have more opportunity to work smart and play hard at learning.

QUESTIONS FOR REFLECTION

1. What do you do to make connections across instruction, curriculum, and life?

2. What brain principles are important for meeting the cognitive and emotional needs of children like John?

3. Regarding the brain-compatible framework for student achievement, how does the feature of effective instruction related to making connections harmonize with the following?

   - Brain-Compatible Principles 1–4: safety, respect, novelty, and memory
   - Core Propositions 2–4: knowledge of subjects and how to teach those subjects; responsibility for managing and monitoring student learning; systematic thinking about best practice and learning from experience

3 Teaching Skills in Multiple Lesson Types

*The key for teachers and for students is empowerment—
the personal empowerment that comes with independence
rather than submissiveness or resentment.*
—Frank Smith, *To Think*

Feature 2

Students learn skills in multiple lesson types.

Students in higher-performing schools learned skills in multiple lesson types. What does the feature look like in the classroom? Chapter 3 answers the question by describing the feature and illustrating how its characteristics complement brain-compatible principles and core propositions of accomplished teaching.

We use the brain-compatible framework for student achievement to see how the feature related to skills instruction harmonizes with

- Brain-Compatible Principles 1–3: safety; respect; novelty;
- Core Propositions 1–2: commitment to students and their learning; knowledge of subject and how to teach those subjects. (See Figure 3.1.)

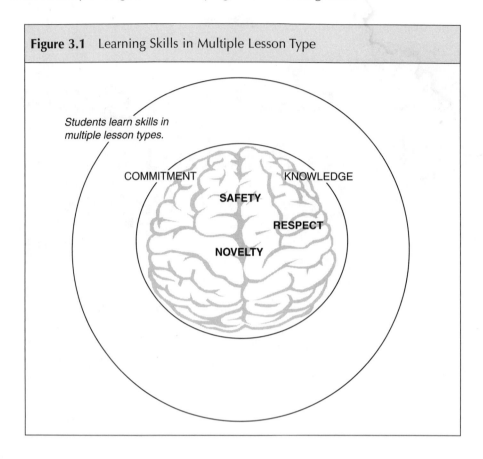

Figure 3.1 Learning Skills in Multiple Lesson Type

Students learn skills in multiple lesson types.

COMMITMENT   KNOWLEDGE

SAFETY

RESPECT

NOVELTY

CHARACTERISTICS OF FEATURE 2

How effective teachers in higher performing schools teach the skills associated with the conventions and mechanics of language is the focus of Feature 2. Research identified three different approaches to skills instruction: *separate*, *simulated*, and *integrated*.

SEPARATE, SIMULATED, AND INTEGRATED INSTRUCTION

Separate instruction is used by *typical* (Langer, 2000, 2004) teachers who rely on textbook practice, skill and drill questions, and tear-out sheets from peripheral workbooks to help them "cover" required curriculum. Simply put, they teach skills in lessons that are contextually isolated from other activities.

Simulated instruction is used by teachers who incorporate within regular units of instruction lessons specifically designed for skills practice. Teachers who rely on the simulated approach routinely prepare their own worksheets, connecting them to whatever language arts activities students might be working on. They locate and use existing materials that invite students to read and write with the purpose of practicing a specific skill embedded in the reading or writing. Students are invited to look for examples of certain skills or concepts in their reading and writing, in school as well as outside. For example, students can be encouraged to find prepositional phrases in newspapers or magazines.

Integrated instruction is used by teachers who foster effective writing skills by expecting students to apply their understanding of skills within purposeful writing activities. For the first-grade teacher, the activity might expect students to include periods at the end of a sentence about their favorite color; for the middle school teacher, correct usage of *there, they're,* and *their* in one paragraph; for the high school teacher, few or no mechanical/usage errors in a research report. Student skills are strengthened within authentic writing activities. For example, short (mini-) lessons are used to remind students of specific rules they have already learned (perhaps in separate lessons), and peer conferences or teacher conferences address editing as well as revision.

Findings (Langer, 2000, 2004) showed that *typical* teachers, those whose students did not perform as well on high-stakes tests as the students of others (termed "successful" and "effective"), relied on the separate approach most of the time. Successful and effective teachers used all three types.

KATIE'S STORY

Katie is a second grader who likes her school and her classroom. She is happy to be in school today with her teacher, because last night her mother had a fight with her boyfriend who hit her. Katie doesn't know how her mommy is or where she is because the police took both her mother and the boyfriend and left Katie with a willing neighbor who took her to school. Katie hopes the man doesn't hit her mommy again. She hopes the police will keep him in jail. She feels ashamed to wear the same dress she had on yesterday. She knows it doesn't smell very good. She doesn't want to be the lunch-line leader today, even though the calendar shows her to be. She is so happy when her teacher asks if she'd like to be the caboose today, and happier still when she is asked to write a sentence telling the teacher what her favorite color is. Katie is pleased that she remembered to put a period at the end of her sentence: My favorite color is yellow. She doesn't feel like drawing a yellow flower. She asks the teacher if she can, instead, put her head on her desk for a few minutes and her teacher says yes.

REFLECTING ON THE BRAIN-COMPATIBLE FRAMEWORK AND FEATURE 2

Let's examine Katie's story from the perspective of the brain-compatible framework for student achievement using words and phrases from the targeted brain-compatible principles, core propositions, and feature.

Katie's teacher is committed *to her students and their learning*. She *cares* about her students deeply. She learned early about Katie's situation and consistently attempts to rescue Katie from thoughts of her unsafe home life, at least during the time she spends with Katie. The teacher respects Katie when, believing she must feel embarrassed by her disheveled appearance, she switches Katie's job to one that honors the little girl while at the same time keeps her out of the eyes of classmates who might criticize her appearance.

Katie's teacher *knows the subject she teaches and how to teach the subject*. She *integrates instruction* as she monitors students' understanding of end punctuation by embedding skill practice within the context of a purposeful activity, namely, students writing a sentence about their favorite color. Even though Katie didn't draw anything yellow, the activity suggests the teacher *respects* the learning style preferences (see Chapter 2) of her students, in this case, her visual-spatial learners who may enjoy the *novelty* of drawing a picture of something with their favorite color as well as identifying it by writing a sentence.

Katie enjoyed her day at school because she was with an effective, brain-compatible teacher whose practice exhibits safety, respect, and novelty and also core propositions and a feature of effective instruction:

- Commitment to students and learning, and knowledge of subject and how to teach the subject
- Effective teaching by embedding in a writing activity the rudimentary skill of using end punctuation correctly

THE BRAIN-COMPATIBLE FRAMEWORK WITH FEATURE 2 IN ACTION

The next section provides a variety of activities that exemplify simulated and integrated instruction. Separate instruction, which relies on existing resources such as textbooks and peripheral workbooks, will not be discussed because the availability of resources varies widely across schools and districts.

Rethinking Daily Skills Warm-Ups

Language arts teachers often start their classes with warm-up activities centered on skills instruction. Separate instruction is exemplified by teachers who use packaged resources that offer daily sentences for students to correct. A better alternative relies on the simulated-instruction approach used by teachers who use sentences their students have written. Regardless of whether the warm-up focuses on spelling, punctuation, capitalization, usage, or syntax, teachers should reconsider what they ask students to do with those sentences.

Most language arts teachers routinely present students with sentences filled with errors of one sort or the other when, if we really want to be brain-compatible teachers, the sentences we put on the board should already be correct!

We need to invite students to examine the correctness of each sentence, that is, to analyze why the spelling, punctuation, capitalization, usage, or syntax is correct. By helping our students visualize and rehearse correctness, we nurture their understanding of correct skills so they are better prepared to identify errors when they present themselves within their own writing, a peer's writing, or a high-stakes test question.

Using correct sentences for daily language-skills instruction is particularly important for our English language learners. Sousa (2006b) discussed the importance of presenting correct information first, the prime remembering time. Language arts teachers might argue that correctness *eventually* emerges from the incorrect sentences with which they challenge students. However, the correctness comes only after the working memories of their students have first seen and heard incorrectness. Imagine the disservice this practice imposes on English language learners trying to learn English. They rightfully assume what their language arts teachers say and write is correct. How confused English language learners must be when they watch fellow students eagerly cross out words and punctuation to *fix* what their teachers presented to them!

Comprehensible Input. Language acquisition scholar Stephen Krashen (2002, 2003) holds that conscious learning of language may work on grammar tests for the short haul, but if we want learners to acquire lasting literacy skills, we must first provide enough *comprehensible input*, that is, correct oral and written examples comparable to the learner's level of understanding. The reading assigned, the writing presented, the directions used should all be comprehensible. If we expect the working memories of students to efficiently identify and process patterns of correct skills into long-term storage, we must no longer rely on outdated skills rituals that warm students up by exposing them to incorrect skills before they have mastered correctness.

I once heard Krashen say that if you give kids enough comprehensible input, the grammar will follow. I agree. Studies on separate grammar instruction suggest that Krashen is correct, that consciously learned competence does not work. The brain learns through repetition. Let's help our students learn language skills by offering repetition in correctness daily. By doing so we will help them learn correctness and better prepare them to identify incorrectness wherever they find it.

Practicing Correctness. Here's an example of how to construct warm-up activities that help students' brains rehearse and practice correctness. This simulated instruction activity directed students to identify and explain why the underlined words and phrases in sentences they had written (in their narratives) were correct. In these sentences, students processed the correctness of capitalization in proper nouns, use of quotation marks, and construction of a complex sentences:

- The <u>Beeline Highway</u> is the fastest way to get to <u>Payson</u>.
- My mother delivered my baby brother at <u>Scottsdale Memorial Hospital.</u>

- He said, "Let her go to the party without me."
- We traveled through many states last summer, and one of them was California.
- My favorite baseball team is the Toronto Blue Jays, even though I live in Arizona.

Delight Diehn (personal communication, January 14, 2008), executive board member and president of *Arizona—Teachers of English to Speakers of Other Languages* (AZ-TESOL), believes activities such as practicing correctness satisfy the needs of English language learners because they offer learners the opportunity to hear many models of correct speaking—both teachers and students—on a daily basis. Practicing correctness benefits English language learners because it reinforces correct grammar and usage on a regular basis. Further, practicing the correctness of grammar allows language learners to see, hear, write, and discuss language skills within the safety of smaller groups or teams and protects them from the uncomfortable and unrealistic challenge of correcting problems within sentences before they have even learned the English language!

Diehn believes ideal environments for English language learners are those where teachers

- celebrate diversity;
- develop meaningful and interesting activities that build on learners' prior knowledge;
- use advance organizers and nonlinguistic representations of learning material, for example, video excerpts or pictorial brochures presented at the beginning of units of study;
- help reduce stress that interferes with learning;
- help increase students' engagement and sense of safety;
- pair or group students with emerging skills with those demonstrating more advanced skills (see Chapters 2 and 7);
- routinely incorporate hands-on projects, graphic organizers, and thinking maps to guide student reading and writing (see *Hero Quest* in Chapter 4).

What Diehn describes as the ideal environment for English language learners should encourage brain-compatible teachers who most likely strive to create and sustain such environmental ideals for all their students. Ultimately, Diehn believes, the single most influential factor to student success is the teacher in the classroom. Brain-compatible teachers will likely agree!

Homework and Literacy Skills

Does homework build literacy skills or tear them down? Can we ensure students are practicing good techniques at home? What support mechanisms are in place to assist students needing help? How do we know whether students do their own homework or copy answers from friends or the Internet? What is the consequence for students who do their own homework but get wrong answers or use poor grammar? How will practicing incorrectness affect the skills proficiency of fledgling writers, especially our English language learners?

If we want to count ourselves among teachers satisfying the three components of the brain-compatible framework for student achievement, we will reflect on critical questions when preparing homework assignments. Homework in the form of skill-and-drill handouts may satisfy parents who clamor for homework; however, such homework does little to satisfy the brain's thirst for novel and interesting activities and little to promote writing skills. As writing coaches we need to plan homework assignments carefully and thoughtfully. Consider this: would a good soccer coach send the team home to practice goal-keeping regardless of a player's skill level or position on the team?

When you assign homework, ask critical questions that help ensure your assignments are compatible with how the brain learns. Consider and accommodate for developmental appropriateness, meaningfulness, safety, and respect. Remember too that students gain a stronger understanding of what good writing looks and sounds like when they discover and produce such work *inside,* not outside, the classroom work environment.

Homework is a valid formative assessment instrument if assigned and graded from a practice-makes-perfect stance, not the 100-percent-or-zero stance of yesteryear. Posting zeros in our gradebooks when students fail to do assignments suggests we espouse to *punishment* assessment, which is neither authentic assessment nor brain friendly. Additionally, assigning too much weight to homework averages (more than 15 percent) also skews the authenticity of our measurement of student performance. (School administrators wondering why some teachers have so many more failing students than others have may want to survey staff regarding the weight they assign to homework assignments, as well as policies related to, for example, makeup work and lateness.)

Editing

Over time, correctness moves from the working memory to long-term storage, increasing the likelihood that, when high-stakes test time approaches, students will be better prepared. When test time rolls around and separate skills instruction may be appropriate, brain-compatible teachers understand that their instruction in skills must capture the enthusiasm of students typically bored by traditional grammar lessons. Having rehearsed and practiced correct skills, they are ready for tests that challenge them to find errors in their writing, within anonymous peer model writing, and ultimately the high-stakes tests that ask them to identify mechanical and syntactical errors.

Educator and researcher Frank Smith (1991), reminiscent of Dewey, wisely argued that students can be trusted to learn as long as they are provided meaningful learning environments that encourage thinking. The brain-compatible framework's editing process, which uses student work to illustrate miscues, provides just such a personalized and meaningful environment.

Thinking Outside the Textbook Box

Brain-compatible teaching may not require additional resources, but it does require thinking outside the textbook box, that is, shifting our frame of reference to look at a common situation in an uncommon way. Brain-compatible teachers, for example, work with (but beyond) textbooks to help their students learn to write.

Proficient writers do not learn to write by completing textbook drills and memorizing lists of vocabulary words. Proficient writers learn to write because they write and write and write. They also read. As William Faulkner (n.d.) suggested, "If you want to become a good writer, read, read, read. . . . Read everything—trash, classics, good and bad, and see how they do it. . . . Then write."

Effective brain-compatible writing teachers use circumstances and issues that affect their learners' lives as writing opportunities. They view textbooks as reference books, one resource among many that helps students understand why and how our language works the way it does.

Vocabulary: A Matter of Relevance

Selecting vocabulary words from the context of reading and writing activities ensures we are teaching skills in the multiple lesson types. For example, we use simulated instruction when we ask students to learn the meaning of words like *fluency*, *relevant*, and *trite*, words regularly appearing in the rubrics used to score their writing (see Chapter 5). I introduce vocabulary words related to writing rubrics early in the year and invite students to create posters that serve as instructional displays throughout the year. The following is a sample of one student's explanation of the vocabulary word *appropriate*, which appears in the writing rubric for word choice:

appropriate (adj.)—suitable

- *A champagne toast was very appropriate for the New Year's Eve celebration.*
- *Be sure the words you use in your writing are appropriate and, hopefully, interesting.*

An example of integrated instruction involving vocabulary might find students using vocabulary words from writing rubrics to support the scores they give their writing during self-assessment activities. For example, one student wrote: "I think my audience will fall asleep if I don't revise many of the *trite* words I have in my first draft. So far I'd give myself a strong 2 but a weak 3 in word choice."

Practicing With Multiple Lesson Types

Experiment with simulated and integrated lessons to discover how the high-interest variety that comes from teaching skills in multiple lesson types fosters student achievement while simultaneously enriching the brain-friendly environment in your classrooms. The following activities are intended to inspire first steps.

Conjunction Grab Bags

To teach students how to expand their sentences from simple to complex, I select a sampling of coordinating conjunctions and *toss* them into a grab bag. I invite students to choose conjunctions from the grab bag and create compound or complex sentences using simple sentences within current writing assignments. I monitor their work as well as invite them to share their work with editing partners. The simulated instruction activity transforms to an integrated activity when I invite students to revise their original piece of writing by replacing simple sentences with compound or complex sentences they recognize as more effective.

Grab bags have the potential to help teachers change from typical teachers to brain-compatible writing teachers and coaches. The change starts when we stop relying exclusively on separate skills lessons (a practice that does not foster student achievement) and start experimenting with simulated and integrated lessons. The unique appearance of the grab bag plus the freedom to choose inherent in grab bag activities help stimulate learner interest by appealing to the novelty brains crave. Moreover, the freedom to choose provided by grab bags enables students to select words or concepts they may find safe, particularly important for English language learners or students needing a little more processing time as they learn particular skills.

Best of all, grab bags work well with students of all ages and content areas. The conjunction grab bag shown illustrates an example of how language arts teachers can prepare simulated lessons on sentence fluency (see writing rubrics, Chapter 6). After presenting the grab bag to students via document camera, overhead projector, whiteboard, or other medium, teachers instruct students to grab conjunctions from the grab bag and use them to expand simple sentences teachers have selected from student writing. To transform the activity into an integrated lesson aimed at helping students develop their sentence fluency, teachers might direct students to review drafts on which they have been working and use conjunctions they grab to revise simple sentences. (Learn more about grab bags in Chapter 6.)

Figure 3.2 Conjunction Grab Bag

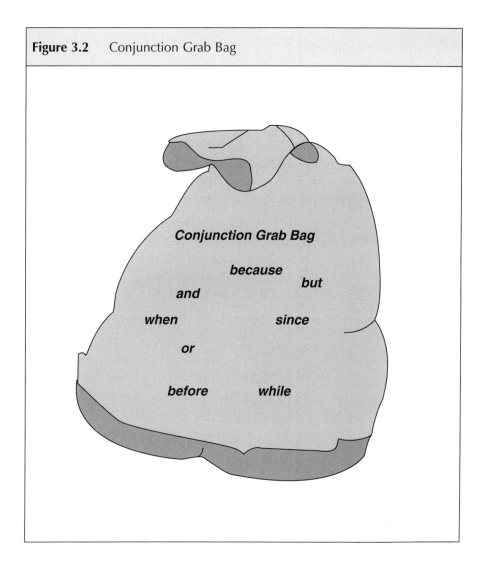

Sentence Savvy

I use students' writing to prepare activities like the following, making sure I first present a short lesson on the skills' rules being covered.

SENTENCE SAVVY: FRAGMENTS

· ·

SENTENCES

As we know, a sentence represents a complete thought.

Examples

> I wrote a poem.
> I sang a song.

Watch out for fragments!

A *fragment* is an incomplete thought.

Examples

> As John wrote his poem.
> While singing a song.

> Don't let the period fool you! An incomplete thought is a fragment—***not*** a sentence. Fragments allow readers to take control away from writers. Readers can conclude anything they want:

> As John wrote his poem, he ate pizza.

Writers take control back from readers when they revise fragments to complete their own thoughts!

> As John wrote his poem, he realized he was using similes and metaphors.

· ·

TRY IT OUT!

Choose a piece of your writing to review for fragments. Working alone or with a partner, identify and correct any fragments you may have written.

Musical Parts of Speech

The following activity invites students to work with the (sometimes very unusual) names of their favorite singing groups.

 MUSICAL PARTS OF SPEECH

Do Now

- Think about at least two of your favorite singers or singing groups.
- Why are the names of these singers and groups proper nouns?

. . . .

USEFUL REMINDERS

Common **nouns** are people, places, and things.
Proper nouns are <u>specific</u> people, places and things.
    They are CAPITALIZED.
Adjectives describe nouns.
Verbs are action words.
Adverbs describe verbs, adjectives, and other adverbs.

. . . .

Try It Out!

- Choose the name of a singing group.
- Identify the parts of speech of the words as they appear in the group's name.
- Write a sentence using words from the singing group's name.
- Identify the parts of speech of the words in the sentence.
- Be careful! The parts of speech might change from the original—function follows form!

EXAMPLE 1

Proper noun: *The Doors*
Original: doors (common noun)
Sentence: The <u>doors</u> (plural noun) in my house are made of brass.

EXAMPLE 2

Proper Noun: *Spice Girls*
Original: spice (adjective) girls (noun)
Sentence: The <u>girls</u> (plural common noun) <u>spiced</u> (verb) up the cookies with ginger.

GROUPS TO CONSIDER OR CHOOSE YOUR OWN!

*The White Stripes • Silverchair • Red Hot Chili Peppers
Goo Goo Dolls • The Wallflowers • The Gorillaz
Tonic • Rage Against the Machine • Garbage • Blur*

Calling All Teachers!

MIDDLE SCHOOL TEACHERS. The sample provided is ideally suited for your students. Encourage them to add their favorite singing groups to a list of examples you have provided. Ask them to identify the various parts of speech within each proper noun.

ELEMENTARY SCHOOL TEACHERS. Invite your students to brainstorm a list of their favorite singing groups. Tell students that each name represents a proper noun because it is a particular person, place or, thing. Have students identify the part of speech of one word within the proper noun and write it on a separate line.

Example
    Proper Noun: Red Hot Chili Peppers
    Common Noun: peppers

HIGH SCHOOL TEACHERS. Challenge students to incorporate their favorite singing groups' names into sentences containing appositives.

Example
    Proper Noun: Red Hot Chili Peppers
    Appositive: one of my favorite groups
    Sentence: I don't believe the rumors that Red Hot Chili Peppers, one of my favorite groups, is breaking up.

Solve the Problem

Toward the end of a unit of skills instruction, teachers are responsible for assessing their students' progress. Before the tests, especially if they are high-stakes tests (and after my students have practiced and rehearsed correctness), I rely on the brain-compatible principle related to novelty by using activities like the one I call *solve the problem.*

☹ ☺ ☺ SOLVE THE PROBLEM! ☹ ☺ ☺

Problem

The sentence bloopers below were borrowed from student writing.

Solution

- **Identify** unclear or confusing statements, misused words, or missing punctuation.
- **Rewrite** each sentence correctly in the space provided.

··

PRIZE-WINNING BLOOPER

Jeff said, "A small white sign was caught in the corner of my eye." (Huh?)

Possible solution: Jeff said, "A small white sign caught my attention."

··

TRY IT OUT!

Rewrite each sentence in a way that expresses what the writers may have been trying to communicate.

1. This one lady came up to me and said, would you like to buy my ticket?
2. Their were many people pushing and shoving there way to the front of the line.
3. I picked up my cupcake and stuffed them into my mouth, and went down to my empty stomach.
4. Wow those were good can I have another?
5 My hand sunk right throw the doe.

QUESTIONS FOR REFLECTION

1. To what extent do you deliver skills instruction in multiple lesson types: separate, simulated, and integrated?

2. How might you modify the way you deliver skills instruction?

3. Regarding the brain-compatible framework for student achievement, how does the feature of effective instruction related to skills instruction harmonize with the following?

   - Brain-Compatible Principles 1–3: safety; respect; novelty
   - Core Propositions 1–2: commitment to students and their learning; knowledge of subject and how to teach those subjects

4 Integrating Test Preparation Into Instruction

Not everything that can be counted counts,
and not everything that counts can be counted.
—Albert Einstein

Feature 3

Teachers integrate test preparation into instruction.

Teachers in higher performing schools integrate test preparation into instruction, a deceivingly simple statement considering NCLB has raised the stakes of testing higher than ever before in history. We will explore the brain-compatible framework for student achievement to see how the third feature, related to the integration of test preparation into instruction, harmonizes with

- Brain-Compatible Principles 1–4: safety; respect; novelty; memory;
- Core Propositions 3–5: responsibility for managing and monitoring student learning; systematic thinking about best practice and learning from experience; commitment to learning community. (See Figure 4.1.)

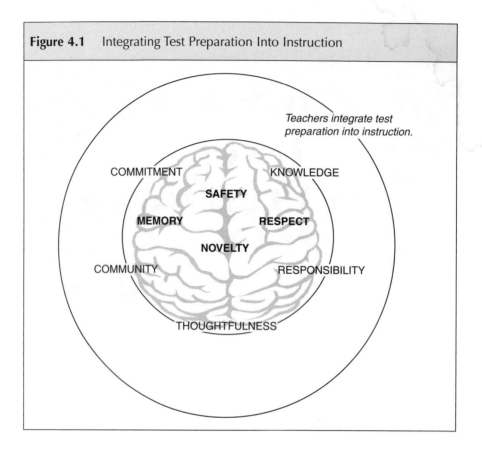

Figure 4.1 Integrating Test Preparation Into Instruction

CHARACTERISTICS OF FEATURE 3'S SUCCESSFUL TEACHERS

The effective teachers who integrate test preparation into instruction are the same successful teachers from Chapters 1 and 2, the teachers who weave skills instruction seamlessly into their lessons and who plan, plan, plan so that students making connections across instruction, curriculum, and life is the norm. Research (Langer, 2000, 2004) showed student achievement on high-stakes tests occurs when teachers are committed to beating the odds (including the odds faced by children of poverty or ethnic minority status). Examples of how effective teachers integrate test preparation into instruction include some or all of the following:

- Designing plans that connect students with their standards and curriculum
- Developing strategies that enable students to build test-taking skills
- Collaborating with colleagues and administrators to study high-stakes test demands/content to assure alignment with curriculum and make adjustments if necessary

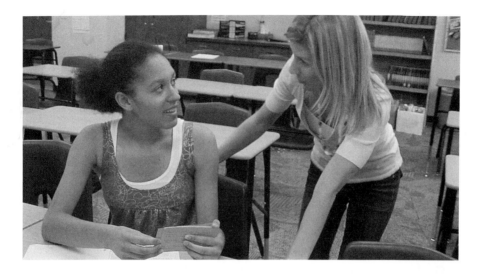

- Analyzing test demands to identify connections to their standards
- Ensuring students are familiar with test format
- Helping students become more reflective about their reading and writing performance using rubrics throughout the year (see Chapter 5)
- Using daily warm-up activities for students to work on independently or with others
- Inviting students to create multiple choice questions similar to those they encounter on tests
- Fostering writing throughout the year

As you can see, the characteristics are plentiful, but they are not prescriptive. Identify those that you feel you can implement, and you will get that much closer to integrating test preparation into your daily instruction so that not only test scores improve but also authentic literacy skills in reading and writing.

ALVARO'S STORY

Alvaro was moved into my classroom from his ESL class after six weeks of school. An extremely polite and respectful young man, he sought and welcomed the opportunity to be in an English-speaking class. Alvaro's mechanical skills were commendable for a newly mainstreamed ESL student. In simple yet eloquent English, he presented strong evidence that he could read literature critically and interpretively. His written work at testing time, however, did not reflect his oral ability. When I announced the district writing test was weeks away, he covered his head with his arms and lay his head in his desk.

REFLECTING ON THE BRAIN-COMPATIBLE FRAMEWORK AND FEATURE 3

You should by now be able to recognize the compatibility of what you know about brain-compatible principles and what you are learning about NBPTS as reflected in the core propositions. Whether you think about student achievement in terms of a feature, a proposition, or a principle, student achievement depends on high-stakes, brain-centered instruction. When it comes to writing achievement, the stakes are even higher. Writing is a literacy-based life skill by which our students will be judged in and out of school.

Intentionally or instinctively, teachers who integrate test preparation into instruction demonstrate an understanding and support of the four brain-compatible principles. Striving to create interesting and challenging activities to sustain authentic learning opportunities supports *novelty*. Inviting students to write throughout the year, and to reflect on their performance and their learning, demonstrates an understanding of the important role *memory* plays in learning. Teachers understand and support the brain-compatible principles of *safety* and *respect* whenever they accept the time and commitment necessary to satisfy the test-preparation feature and every other feature as well. Feel confident that you uphold brain-compatible principles, satisfied in the knowledge they are backed by research-based best practices.

Similarly, NBPTS propositions regarding commitment, subject knowledge, systematic thinking, managing, and monitoring are reflected in the examples and actions of Feature 3's effective teachers. (Teachers satisfy Proposition 5 when they collaborate with district or site leaders and colleagues to ensure the proper alignment of curricula.)

THE BRAIN-COMPATIBLE FRAMEWORK WITH FEATURE 3 IN ACTION

As brain-compatible writing teachers, we must delve more deeply into the consciousness of our students and into the writing process itself. Writing involves every one of our senses. We touch the pen, pencil, keyboard. We hear and see words scratched onto paper, clicked onto a screen. Sights, sounds, scents, tastes—real and imagined—morph into the writer's words. Direct experience with the writing process teaches us that writing is a very active, erratic, impulsive, and recursive process, and a traditional textbook version of the alleged five stages of the writing process (prewriting, brainstorming, composing rough drafts, revising, editing, and writing a final copy) falls short of what we need to know.

- How do we encourage students to write on a regular basis, regardless of their skill level or comfort with the language, so they will perform well on test days rather than give up?
- How do we move students toward mastery while adhering to the testing timelines imposed on us?
- How do we balance students' learning needs with the needs of the school principal, the district, and the state?
- How can we authentically assess learners in an environment invaded by standardized writing tests?

Let's explore brain-compatible examples that measure up to the standards of the effective teachers whose integration of test preparation into instruction *beat the odds* (Langer, 2000) stacked against their students' success. Remember, nothing suggested in this book is prescriptive. Implement only the research-based changes that make sense to you, keeping your students' achievement in mind. Study your resources (e.g., textbooks, ancillary reading materials, curriculum guides, standards) in relation to the tests your students take, and prepare an initial "road map" or "mind map" that outlines the highlights of every unit you are planning in relation to the overarching standards on which your students will be assessed.

- Create a framework that complements the types of writing you will be addressing and assessing. Identify an order to deliver your instruction that aligns logically with federally mandated state and district tests. As writing coaches we may want to scaffold our lessons by introducing description and narration before the more complex exposition and persuasion. Unfortunately, we must be ready to accept that testing mandates were not designed by teachers and may warrant the instruction of exposition or persuasion first.
- Identify your standards-based and curriculum-based teaching goals in concise and measurable terms that you, your students, and your principal will understand. If you teach younger students, you may want to consider writing the state standard on the board in words they will understand, for example, "At the end of class, I will be able to . . . ."
- Identify short stories and student writing samples you can incorporate into reading and writing lessons that reflect tested objectives. Plan vocabulary lessons that use words embedded in the texts students read. Learning how to decode words from contextual clues in context will help students far more on high-stakes tests than memorizing the spelling and meaning of shopping lists of words taken from such-and-such workbook. By the way, research on the six fea-

tures of effective instruction showed that prepackaged materials marketed to one district to improve test scores did not match the test very well, not to mention the learning needs of the students. If vocabulary workbooks are mandated, incorporate the required words into planned activities that use the prescribed words in meaningful, engaging ways. (See "The Open Boat" vocabulary lesson in Chapter 6.)

● Encourage and assist students (if necessary) to look up unfamiliar terms as they present themselves in the dictionary. Often students are permitted to use dictionaries and thesauri during testing situations. If they have not learned how to use them, they will be fooled into thinking they should try, only to find themselves wasting precious minutes of testing time.

● Remember, the first feature of effective instruction recommends teaching skills in multiple-type lessons. Try to minimize the amount of separate skills lessons you use so that you and students do not suffer through textbook exercises that promise little in the way of transferable writing skills.

- Identify proficient and exemplary student samples for each writing type you will be introducing (e.g., fictional narrative, persuasive essay). Incorporate them into learning activities throughout the term. Help students build their skills naturally by permitting them to read and read often and to rehearse grammar skills by identifying correctness (versus incorrectness) on a daily basis so that when high-stakes tests ask them to write, they have a better chance to write correctly. When students are asked to identify grammatical errors, they will have a better chance at succeeding because their brains will have had more opportunities to hardwire correctness.

- Create a planning calendar (see Chapter 2) that provides a big-picture snapshot of the whole term or year as well as weekly snapshot of goals. By letting students know where they are heading, they stand a better chance of getting there.

- Locate visually stimulating photos, posters, charts, overheads, and graphics to support each unit of learning. Identify relevant music, manipulatives, field trips, and other sensory tools and strategies to engage multiple learning pathways. Change peripherals often to maintain a novel, engaging brain-friendly environment that continually connects activities to purposeful objectives.

- Encourage questions and feedback, and conduct brief mind-mapping activities that tap into learners' full (logical and creative) brain potential. Focus on free expression and process-oriented learning. Ask volunteers to share their mind maps with the rest of the group.

> Because neurons thrive only in an environment that stimulates them to receive, store, and transmit information, our challenge as educators is simply to define, create, and maintain an emotionally and intellectually stimulating school environment and curriculum.
>
> —Robert Sylwester

When we integrate into our lesson plans multiple modes of communication (e.g., reading, speaking, listening, media viewing), we form strong foundations for effective writing. And when a lesson is so well planned that it engages students' brains in (seemingly) effortless ways, good behavior, fun, and learning inevitably happen. These are the building blocks to learning success that marry brain-compatible classroom principles to research-based features and propositions shown to positively influence student achievement on high-stakes tests.

TEST SAVVY

By planning to include test instruction regularly, we will help ourselves avoid the pitfalls faced by typical teachers who, frazzled by the imminent high-stakes test, become irritable, succumbing to impatience, sarcasm, and cynicism that poorly mask the teacher frustration and dissatisfaction associated with high-stakes testing (e.g., Abrams & Madaus, 2003; Clarke, et al., 2003; Moon, Callahan, & Tomlinson, 2003).

Planning to incorporate test instruction into our practice eases our stress and allows us to be patient with learners who are struggling with various concepts. If we scold or criticize learners, they naturally abandon cortical learning plans and retreat to fight-or-flight plans. When teachers lose their patience and forget they are the adults, they risk pushing their learners into the fight-or-flight responses of misbehavior or indifference. Sarcasm, that often alleged form of humor, will similarly push learners into their flight-or-fight mode. (Robbing teachers of the trusting bond between teacher and learner, sarcasm has nothing to do with humor. Sarcasm is not defined as humor in any dictionary.)

The writing experience can be joyful or painful, but preparing for high-stakes writing tests often means the latter more than the former. We, therefore, need to let our learners know, and know early, that we know the pain connected with writing as well as the joy. We need to let our learners know that whatever emotions we may experience while writing, writing requires revising, revising, and revising. Patience and mutual support will help you and your learners avoid getting testy about the test.

By embedding test preparation into our daily routines, we will help ease students' test anxiety. We set up classroom environments whereby we encourage them to learn from mistakes, rather than shy away from them. By planning and delivering integrated, authentically assessed units of language arts instruction, we demonstrate we are effective, accomplished brain-compatible teachers.

Maintaining challenging but realistic standards holds learners accountable in a respectable manner. When introducing competition into peer activities, we make sure those activities foster cooperation among students rather than instigate frustration and resentment. If we view ourselves as coaches, gearing players up for the big (test) game, we can help students manage their stress, using it as a motivation to prepare and succeed.

A research-based way to prepare learners for high-stakes tests is to have them take mock tests in class that reflect the format of the real thing (see "Before and After High-Stakes Tests Formats"). For example, get students used to the pattern and procedure of answering questions. Will they be expected to circle the correct answer on the test itself or to pencil in a corresponding bubble on a separate answer sheet? What should they do if they don't know the answer? How much time should they spend on a question? Have students practice answering questions, penciling in the bubbles, erasing answers, and deciding what to do with a question when they don't know the answer. Such practice reduces the mental stress that can occur under pressure.

Practice, especially under voluntary and motivated circumstances, sets up the brain for meaningful learning by converting information from short- to long-term memory. Practice also lessens the brain's fear or anxiety response to the unknown and strengthens the neural connections that are formed while learning and receiving feedback.

Embedding test practice into daily instruction so it disappears into engaging activities fosters a *sí puedo* (yes, I can) attitude in students that should not be underestimated. A positive attitude is known to virtually alter the chemistry of the brain, fostering the production of dopamine, a "feel-good" neurotransmitter that propels optimism, and noradrenalin, which provides physical energy to act upon motivations. Ultimately, attitude influences the activation of the frontal lobes, which are responsible for long-term planning and judgment.

Testy on Test Day?

Have you ever lost patience with students who treat their test booklets and answer sheets like coloring books? You know the students I mean: the ones who darken bubble-sheet circles according to the decorative patterns

BEFORE AND AFTER
HIGH-STAKES TEST FORMATS

Before High-Stakes Tests Format. Proofreading Skills: Identify the correct word choice.

1. Please don't _____ the pipe at the boy.
    (a) throw   (b) through
2. The deputies took _____ father to jail because he took the food.
    (a) their   (b) there   (c) they're

After High-Stakes Tests Format. Proofreading Skills
Directions: Read each sentence carefully. If one of the words in the sentence is misspelled, misused, or not capitalized correctly, mark the space for that word. If all the underlined words are correct, then mark the space for No mistake.

1. Please <u>don't</u> <u>through</u> the pipe at the <u>boy</u>. No mistake.
         A   B   C   D

2. The <u>deputies</u> took <u>they're</u> father to jail because he <u>stole</u> food. No mistake.
         F   G   H   J

Before High-Stakes Tests Format. Usage Problems: Rewrite the underlined word or phrase correctly.

1. The boy <u>shoud of went</u> to town with his mother.

After High-Stakes Tests Format. Mechanical Skills
Directions: Read the following taken from project diaries. Notice that each sentence is numbered. Groups of words or punctuation are underlined. The questions ask about the underlined words in each identified sentence.

The boy <u>shoud of went</u> to town with his mother. (1)

1. In sentence (1) <u>shoud of went</u> should be written—
    (a) should of went   (b) should have went
    (c) should have gone   (d) as it is

they visualize to keep them at least somewhat engaged, not the correctness of answers they deduce. To help us fight our frustration rather than our students, we may want to rely on our compassion for students who don't like high-stakes tests any more than we do. Who can blame them, especially if they are students who have been labeled failures for their poor performance on previous tests?

Sending resistant students to the office may satisfy our fighting amygdalae, but not our goals to build safe and respectful classroom environments. Let's consider a possible brain-friendly alternative where we remain in our cortices rather than flee to our amygdalae.

Upon observing a student bubbling in answers arbitrarily (or drawing designs in the margins, and so on), we approach the student slowly, lean over, and whisper something like this: "Excuse me. What's up? I notice you're bubbling in a way that tells me you may not be reading the passages (or problems, and so on) very carefully." Before the student responds, we continue calmly and softly: "I know taking this test is the last thing in the world you'd rather be doing, but I'd like you to consider reading the directions and trying. I know there are questions you can answer. What do you think?"

If the student complies, terrific: we will have modeled patience and acted the adult. Students are not yet capable of acting in an adult manner because their cortices are still developing. If the student does not comply, we can plan to report the incident or try one more time, calmly: "I notice you're continuing your doodles. You can continue doodling if you want, but I will be obliged to report the incident. Another option is for you to read the directions and try your best, which I think is the better alternative. It's your call."

By controlling our instinct to fight resisters, by remembering the brain-compatible principles of safety and respect, we demonstrate our efforts to maintain a caring relationship with our students. If we fail to do so, we risk forfeiting the safe and respectful relationship we have nurtured to support tests in which we may have as little interest as our students. Even under circumstances where we must send belligerent or argumentative students from classrooms out of consideration for the safety and respect and success of other students, we must do so firmly yet calmly, modeling in the best possible way for the learning minds seated before us.

Before the Essay Test: Play!

No matter how young or old your students, the *Hero Quest* strategy represents the serious business of playing. *Hero Quest* is an adventure game that extends learners' enthusiasm for playing to the hard work of writing an essay.

The prize for those who prevail in *Hero Quest* is a cohesive organization of ideas critical to essay writing. *Hero Quest* represents a powerful tool for mapping a writing plan or outline quickly, which becomes especially important when writing tests have time limits. Used in or beyond the language arts classroom, its graphic orientation is especially helpful for visual learners. Planning a response visually provides many learners with a sense of security. They draw a head and think about what they want to say. They draw a torso and understand that a solidly constructed body of support is necessary. They draw the legs and are reminded to ground their responses with a conclusion. For many learners, *Hero Quest* becomes their organizational strategy of choice once they've experienced success with it.

● ●

HERO QUEST

The game is relatively simple. Students identify a "hero" or favorite character from an assigned or chosen reading. With colored markers they draw a graphic representation of their hero and apply pertinent characteristics and qualities.

Some students will prefer to draw their own hero figures; others may choose a preprinted version as illustrated on the next pages. Either way, ultimately, their heroes represent an effectively organized outline for an essay in response to a literary work.

Organization is one of the critical rubrics used to assess proficiency in writing and is recognized as such by groups as small as local school districts and as large as The *Nation's Report Card* organization, the National Assessment for Educational Progress (NAEP). Here is a complete version of the unit I call *Hero Quest*.

Unit Summary

Objectives

1. Students learn to construct an organized outline that guides their subsequent essay writing.

2. Students develop expository writing skills across disciplines. This version of the game focuses on outlining and writing an essay in response to a literary work, a typical language arts objective nationwide. However, it can easily be adapted to any other topic or content area.

Age Appropriateness

Teachers of students from fourth grade to high school have told me their students have used the *Hero Quest* outline with little or no instruction. The unit, as presented, was designed for sixth through ninth graders of any skill level. *Hero Quest* is an especially effective tool for learners with a visual/spatial learning-style preference and for struggling readers and writers. With little modification the unit can be customized for other younger or older groups.

Materials and Resources

Hero Quest activity sheets, teacher's guide, overhead transparencies (optional), and student samples.

Methodology

- Use teacher-facilitated whole- and small-group instruction: students can work alone, in pairs, or in cooperative groups.
- Student responses can be written directly onto a teacher-tailored *Hero Quest* outline or on the student's own hero outline. (Monitor this stage closely. Students sometimes draw figures that are too small to fit all they want to write in their outlines, making them difficult to read.)
- Students compose essays based on their completed outlines that contain an introduction, body, and conclusion.

The Plan

- Provide learners with a reading choice from a number of appropriate options. The following example is based on the reading of an *abridged* version of "The Fall of the House of Usher" by Edgar Allen Poe (Amsco Publications, 1975).

- Distribute copies of the *Hero Quest* instructions and outline sheet. Use visually appealing handouts or overheads to review the instructions as a class before getting started.

One student's
Hero Quest drawing

- Use whole- and small-group instruction and individual assistance while the game plays out and outlines are constructed, transferred, and transformed to essay drafts.

YOUR NOBLE QUEST FOR A HERO

Before your adventure begins, think about the characters you want to
have join you in your quest. Identify at least four characters and write
their names in the area provided below. Also include the name of the
book or movie that inspired each character. One of your characters will
join you in your ultimate *Hero Quest*.

Character	Where did you meet this character?
1.	1.
2.	2.
3.	3.
4.	4.

Once you've named four characters, discuss their traits and characteristics with other learners. Why did you choose these characters? Why do
you admire them? Is there anything about them that you don't like?
What? Why did your classmates choose their specific characters?

_____

_____

_____

_____

_____

_____

_____

_____

_____

_____

_____

_____

_____

_____

THE QUEST

You've identified at least four characters for your upcoming adventure. You've read about them in a book or gotten to know them in a movie. But at the moment, they are trapped in the strange world of "Vague"—a make-believe land where they're vanishing because everything is so terribly vague.

The good news is there's still time to save your characters. So far, only their arms have faded to a blur. Your quest is to rescue *one* hero from the world of "Vague." To do this you must retrieve his/her arms. Once you rescue your main character, he/she will be able to save the others.

Good luck with your mission!

Rescuing Your Main Character

✏ Using either your own hero outline or the one provided, write the name of your main character—the one you wish to rescue—in the head area of your hero.

✏ Write the title of the book or movie where you first met this character directly below his/her name.

Notes: _____

_____

_____

_____

_____

_____

_____

_____

_____

_____

_____

_____

YOUR *HERO QUEST* FIGURE

TATTOOING YOUR HERO

As you enter the world of "Vague" where the vanishing body parts are secretly stored, find your character's arms. *Be careful!* Each arm has a quality tattooed on it! If you don't select the tattoos that best describe the personality of your hero, his or her arms will vanish once again! If you discover the quality you want is not listed here, great! You're thinking creatively. Go ahead and create your own tattoo.

smart   loving   courageous   determined

brave   cruel   conceited   careless

selfish   strong   kind   terrified

curious   thoughtful   lazy   inconsiderate

prejudiced   devoted   compassionate   hard-working

✆ Defend your choices! In order to succeed, think about what your character has done that demonstrates his or her unique qualities. Write some phrases or statements that support your choices in your hero's body area. Do not proceed to the next step until you *know* that you can defend any challenges against your statements. Otherwise, you jeopardize the mission!

✆ Once you have successfully secured your character's arms, write his/her tattooed traits in the head area of your hero as well.

LEGS TO STAND ON

Congratulations. . . . Your character is almost free to leave the strange world of "Vague." If the qualities you've chosen are accurate and can be defended, your hero will survive. However, before your hero can be released from the land of "Vague," he or she needs legs to stand on.

☞   To do this, restate the information in the head of your hero to his or her legs. Once this is done, you will have completed your first quest! Congratulations! The next step is to use the hero you've created toconstruct an essay outline.

Here's a visual example of the steps described:

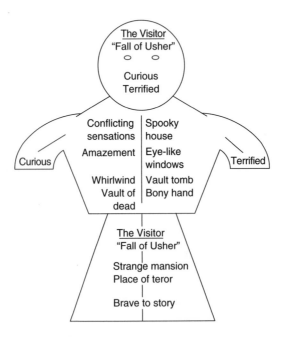

The Visitor
"Fall of Usher"
○   ○
Curious
Terrified

Curious

Conflicting sensations	Spooky house
Amazement	Eye-like windows
Whirlwind Vault of dead	Vault tomb Bony hand

Terrified

The Visitor
"Fall of Usher"
Strange mansion
Place of teror
Brave to story

This example was created by a seventh grader in response to an abridged (grade-level appropriate) version of Poe's classic "The Fall of the House of Usher."

YOUR HERO WRITES

Now, to transform your hero into an essay, follow the steps below:

✐   Write an introduction that states the purpose of your essay. To do this, ask yourself a central question to prompt a response. For example, the student writer in "The Fall of the House of Usher" asked, why was the visitor afraid?

✐   Next, "arm" your essay thesis with sentences that support your hero's tattooed personality traits.

✐   Finally, write a conclusion that restates the essay's purpose, "Stand" your essay on solid ground by restating your introduction. You can include an opinion you expressed about the topic in your conclusion, but avoid using the firstperson voice.

Essay Introduction Example

The Visitor in "The Fall of the House of Usher" finds that his intense curiosity for a dilapidated mansion leads him into a Tomb of Terror.

Play to Prepare

No matter what type of writing students are asked to create, they need to learn how to organize their thoughts. Sometimes, as with timed tests, they must organize their thoughts quickly as well as effectively. Once deemed a boring or tiring activity, organizational outlining becomes an engaging and interesting activity because *Hero Quest* encourages students to play hard at acquiring the important skill and trait of organization in writing.

I encourage you to allow students to experiment with the designs of their *Hero Quest* figures. They will discover the shapes they draw will change along with essay objectives. Practicing with armed and armless heroes helps students visualize and construct plans for their essays. Because student designs take shape based on the needs of their essay quests, comparison/ contrast essays may find students' heroes armless, with multiple circles resembling a Venn diagram in the stomach region.

To promote higher-level thinking (see Chapter 6), invite students to analyze the essays of others and construct *Hero Quest* outlines based on the organization suggested by the finished products. For example, ask students: "What was the writer's mission? The essay's purpose? What traits or characteristics did the author use as tattoos? How did the author conclude and justify the stated mission?" Challenge readers to work with writers to improve the essays, especially if their outlines revealed organizational gaps in the writers' essays.

Student Samples

The four student hero outlines and essays that follow demonstrate the versatility and effectiveness of the *Hero Quest* approach to organization. You'll notice that the subjects range from science to social studies.

- Essay 1 is well organized and demonstrates a grasp of essay technique.
- Essay 2, by contrast, demonstrates that students sometimes write solid outlines but fail to apply the outlines to their essays, providing useful information to teachers on where to go next to help the student.
- Essay 3 demonstrates how revisions are an important step in the process of producing a clearly written and well-organized finished product.
- Essay 4, while exhibiting solid scientific knowledge, demonstrates gaps in essay organization and technique.

Hero Quest can help teachers identify gaps in understanding and application so they can remediate *before* students face high-stakes frustration and potential failure. Regardless of subject matter, we can help students acquire more proficiency in writing by helping them learn the importance of visually organizing their writing and the strategies to do so. What better way to authentically assess students' formative writing than by seeing the organizational pictures they rely on to assist their writing.

Essay 1

JUSTINE'S *HERO QUEST*

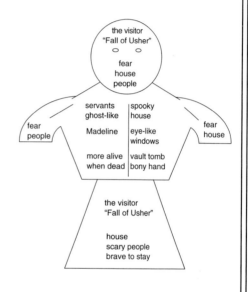

Would you stay in a house if you thought "the Bony Hand of Death" was heading for it? The visitor in "The Fall of the House of Usher" by Edgar A. Poe did just that! In many ways the visitor proved to the reader he was full of fear. Yet, in spite of his fear of the house and the people in it, he stayed with his friend, Roderick Usher.

The house of Usher was no ordinary house. The visitor told about its "vacant eyelike window" which made the house seem real. He was really afraid when he discovered they buried family members right there in the house. He was even more afraid when he discovered that chamber was right underneath the room wherehe stayed!

Not only did the house frighten the visitor, its "tenants" did too. When he looked at Lady Madeline after she had died, she looked more alive in her coffin than when she was alive. He also thought she was a ghost when he first saw her because she moved so oddly; she would move, stand still a long while and then move again. After Usher dies and the visitor tries to give orders to the servants, they ignore him. He was so afraid, he was convinced he was the only living thing in the house.

The visitor in "The Fall of the House of Usher" was full of fear. Not just because of the house but the people too. He was very brave for staying in the house in spite of his fear. Not too many people would do that.

Reproduced as written by student, including errors.

Essay 2

CLAYTON'S *HERO QUEST*

This essay is about the story, "The Fall of the House of Usher." The main character was the visitor. Other characters were Lady Madeline and Roderick Usher.

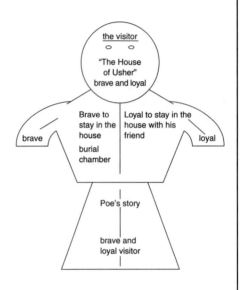

The visitor was loyal to his friend to stay even though he thought that everyone was a ghost.

The visitor was brave because his room was above the burial chamber. He was also brave because he thought that the house was haunted and everyone in it as well.

In conclusion, Lady Madeline dies supposedly and so does Roderick. The visitor got on his horse and rode off he looked back and he saw the house fall apart.

Note: Although, this student did not follow his *Hero Quest* outline, the good news is that remedial action is far easier because he wrote a marginal but adequate outline. I would point out that the introductions don't match, and that Clayton's essay introduction reads more like a plot summary! The two body paragraphs have potential but are not developed. The last paragraph, like the first. Succumbs to the problematic student habit of writing a plot summary, rather than an essay.

I would encourage a consolidation of the two qualities into one–loyalty being the more effective, since the visitor's bravery is the causal effect of his loyalty. Focusing on loyalty will also help the student develop the body paragraph. Next, the teacher can encourage the student to revise the essay and check it against the outline to ensure that they match.

Reproduced as written by student, including errors.

Meet Alvaro

The next example demonstrates the effectiveness of the *Hero Quest* approach with English language learners. In this case students chose from a number of prompts to complete a district writing-assessment test based on a literary selection. As per typical state guidelines, the essay needed to satisfy specific rubrics in writing. Each student received the rubric chart and was directed to assess his or her own draft against the rubric chart before peer conferencing. The test was administered the last week of the second quarter.

I served as Alvaro's conference partner during the essay test. After reading his draft about the boy and mother from *Sounder* (Armstrong, 1969), I recognized that he had written a plot summary that included episodes from the movie, not the book version of the story. When I examined his *Hero Quest* outline, I could not understand much of it, so I asked him to read it to me while I corrected the misspelled words. Through this process I realized that his outline did address the prompt as it related to the book, and it clearly demonstrated a commendable analysis of the *Sounder* character. I praised Alvaro and coached him to write another draft and, this time, to follow his well-prepared outline.

After conferencing with Alvaro, he wrote a similar, neater (bless his heart) version of the original draft. At this point I remained patient and resolved. I accepted that I might not have communicated with him effectively. I risked speaking in the limited Spanish I was learning since joining an English as a Second Language team of teachers. I balanced the possibility of better understanding against the possibility that speaking Spanish would insult Alvaro. He was proud of being in an English-speaking classroom. When I began speaking in Spanish, his eyes grew sorrowful, but he listened intently nonetheless. I told him through words and gestures to try again to follow his good outline. To simplify the assignment, I told him to write only on the courage of the boy, rather than on both the boy and the mother, which would require more examples. I also told him it was okay to use examples from the movie as well as the book because Alvaro had mentioned he'd really enjoyed the movie version.

The outline includes my revisions after conferencing with Alvaro. I wrote the reminder about a conclusion and added the arrow to visually help him.

ESSAY PROMPT

Sometimes love and courage help people to survive when terrible things happen to them. The mother and son in *Sounder* by William Armstrong survive the horrors of racism because of their love and courage. In a well-constructed essay, describe how the mother and the son show their love and courage. Be sure to use specific examples from the novel to support your answer.

Essay 3

ALVARO'S *HERO QUEST*

Alvaro's work is based on the story *Sounder*, a teenage classic written by William Armstrong. It follows a loving family of sharecroppers determined to survive the racism of their time after the father is imprisoned for 6 years for stealing food to feed his family.

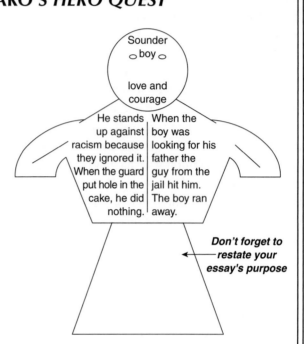

First Draft

One day the father went to work and he disappeared. Nobody from his family knew what or where he has gone. His son went to look for him and found a jail. When the guard looked at him the guard hit him and chased the boy away. After all that the boy found a school. The teacher told him to come in. She was very nice. After school was over the teacher gave him a book and the boy took it home. The boy told his mother. The next day they were working on the farm when Sounder returned and everybody was happy. Then the boy heard someone screaming. He noticed that it was his dad. They were all happy. The next day the boy's father wanted to take him shopping, and the boy didn't want to go. Since that day they were living happy . . .

Reproduced as written by student, including errors.

Note. Spelling corrections have been made in the following example for ease of reading.

Alvaro's Essay Revision

The boy from Sounder showed his courage. He ignored other people that were making fun of him. The boy was always good to other people but the other kids were not good to him. When he found the school one boy told a story of other kids, and they just laughed at him. The boy stood up for him. He said that he believed what he said.

Another way that the boy showed courage was when he was taking the cake to his father and the guard pushed holes in the cake and the boy ignored this.

Note: Alvaro's final draft successfully recounted three incidents (two from the book and one from the movie) that demonstrated the boy's courage.

Hero Quest clearly assisted Alvaro and continues to assist ESL students and other challenged learners who benefit from a clear road map—navigating them away from plot summaries and towards original responses.

Reproduced as written by student, including errors.

Writing Prompt: How is science related to the arts?

Essay 4

SANDY'S ESSAY

I believe science, art, writing, and creativity are very much related to each other in many ways. In this essay I will show you how they are related and why. I will talk about famous people like Leonardo Devinci, Darwin, Copernicus, and Kepler, who used all of these skills to make a break-through in technology. So, sit back and enjoy!

Science, writing, and creativity are related. Creativity relates to everything because all great things start with an idea, like Copernicus and his idea that the Earth revolved around the sun and not the other way around. Gallileo was also very creative and attempted each time something was proven, to investigate the claim to find out if it was true himself.

Art, for many scientists, helps paint the picture of the solution, or in some cases, the problem. DeVinci drew the first pictures of cirrhosis of the liver, as well as muscles, blood vessels, and nerves in the arms. His whole study of the human body was inspired by his perfectionism in art and his need for his sculptures to be perfect. But still many people use art as a way of showing information and facts, like Copernicus showed his thought that the Earth moved around the sun.

Writing is also part of the big picture. All mankind throughout history has written his thoughts, ideas, notes, accomplishments, and much, much more in order to remember. All scientists write down their findings and later on go back, relate similarities, compare differences and come up with a solution. Many people also write down their findings in the books to share with others the information they have acquired, like Kepler and his book, "The New Astronomy" on how Mars made an elliptical orbit. Even Darwin's grandfather, Erasmus Darwin, wrote a long poem on his work as a physician.

In conclusion, I hope you now see that science relates to writing, art, and creativity in many ways. We write things down in order to remember, compare, and contrast our findings. Writing is a vital necessity to science and life. Art is related to science in the way that some things are better drawn and can paint the picture for the reader in a way that words cannot. Creativity is related to science because all ideas start out as creativity. I hope you now agree with me that science, art, writing, and creativity all relate to each other in one way or another.

Note: Although Sandy's essay demonstrates a sound understanding of science content, it could benefit from an organizational revision. As a writing teacher how might you work with this student to help her strengthen the essay's organization?

Reproduced as written by student, including errors.

Drawing a Kinesthetic Connection

Hero Quest represents just one of many organizing tools that can be used throughout the year. Rather than force students to use a particular organizing strategy, introduce a variety of them, for example, thinking maps, and let students decide which is most suitable for their particular needs.

I encourage you to use the following kinesthetic activity to help students remember the steps involved in the *Hero Quest* adventure. Invite students seated at their desks or tables to think about standing up. Say to them: "Stand up. Don't actually stand up! Just think about it. In your mind, picture how you plan to stand up. Will you press both hands to the desk to support you? Will you twist around in your seat or slide out from the side?

"Now that you have thought about it, go ahead and stand up. You've just mimicked the effective organization of an essay. You thought about what it was you were going to do, you considered the support you would need, and then you did it. You stood yourself on solid ground."

Dr. Carol Kessner, an inspiring graduate school professor I once had, shared some valuable advice about writing a thesis that I've repeated to students throughout my career because the advice holds true whether we are writing an essay, research paper, or dissertation: Say what you're going to do, do it, and then say you did it!

QUESTIONS FOR REFLECTION

1. Why is the *Hero Quest* adventure compatible with the intent of Feature 3: Teachers integrate test preparation into instruction?

2. What steps have you taken or might you take to integrate test preparation into instruction?

3. Regarding the brain-compatible framework for student achievement, how does the feature of effective instruction related to integrating test preparation into instruction harmonize with

   - Brain-Compatible Principles 1–4: safety; respect; novelty; memory?
   - Core Propositions 3–5: responsibility for managing and monitoring student learning; systematic thinking about best practice and learning from experience; commitment to learning community?

5 Teaching Students Strategies for Doing the Work

Written language is for ideas, action, reflection, and experience. It is not for having your ignorance exposed, your sensitivity bruised, or your ability assessed.

—Frank Smith, *To Think*

Feature 4

Students learn strategies for doing the work.

Chapter 4 explores how teachers help students learn strategies for doing the work. Continuing our use of the brain-compatible framework for student achievement, we will look at how Feature 4 harmonizes with

- Brain-Compatible Principles 1–4: safety; respect; novelty; memory;
- Core Proposition 3: responsibility for managing and monitoring student learning. (See Figure 5.1.)

CHARACTERISTICS OF FEATURE 4

Students learn strategies for doing the work because their teachers design models and guides that lead students to understand how they should approach each task. Students learn strategies for doing the work because their teachers

Figure 5.1   Learning Strategies For Doing The Work

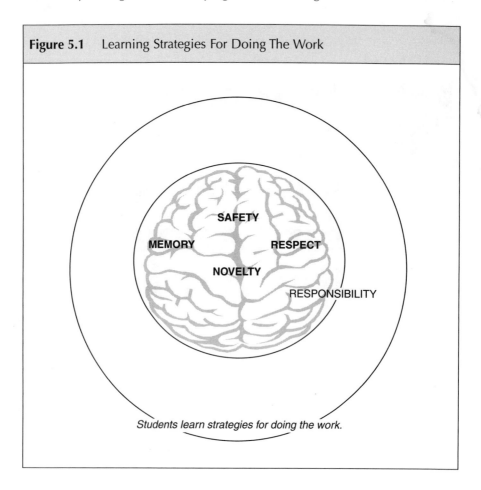

Students learn strategies for doing the work.

give them resources and activities that foster their thinking processes. Research on beating the odds showed that effective language arts teachers in schools with higher performing students used rubrics to help students reflect on their own progress as readers and writers. They invited students to help them develop the rubrics by which they would be scored so that the rubrics, which were used throughout the year, became more meaningful to them.

Effective teachers in the higher performing schools provided models for their students so they could see how to complete a task. They prepared and offered models and reminder sheets that offered students support while working independently to accomplish tasks and asked them to rate their progress.

The research on student achievement showed the effective teachers who beat the odds (Langer, 2000) scaffolded learning activities in a way that ensured students had developed an understanding of a concept before asking them to apply that understanding to more complex activities.

REFLECTING ON THE BRAIN-COMPATIBLE FRAMEWORK AND FEATURE 4

The third core proposition of NBPTS (2007) states that accomplished teachers are responsible for managing and monitoring student learning. The proposition is satisfied by effective teachers who provide models, samples, and rubrics intended to help students learn strategies to become better writers, readers, and thinkers. (NBPTS standards specific to teachers of early adolescence/English language arts articulate specific ways accomplished teachers manifest the core propositions within their practices. For example, the standard for writing includes the board's expectation that teachers provide instruction that ensures success in writing across genres, purposes, and audiences.)

Helping students learn the strategies to do the work is fully supported by brain-compatible teaching as well. In "The Art of Changing the Brain," Zull (2004) reflected on the importance of giving up trying to explain concepts to our students. Explaining tunes them out. Providing engaging activities tunes students in to positive emotions that emerge as learners generate their own ideas, helping to make learning experiences memorable.

Further, readers will see how the characteristics of effective and accomplished teachers are similar to those of brain-compatible teachers who follow principles related to safety, respect, novelty, and memory.

THE BRAIN-COMPATIBLE FRAMEWORK WITH FEATURE 4 IN ACTION

In the following section, I deconstruct one of my lessons and invite readers to *learn the strategies to do the work* necessary to make brain-compatible high-stakes classroom a reality. I believe the lesson demonstrates the five NBPTS core propositions and standards (see Table 5.1) that guide my early adolescence/English language arts certification. I believe, too, the lesson demonstrates characteristics of Feature 4 (and other features) as well as the four brain-compatible principles, and in so doing celebrates the fun, challenges, and learning that occur when teachers work within the brain-compatible framework for student achievement.

THE CLUE TO EXACT WRITING

You are a sixth-grade teacher preparing your students for an upcoming writing assessment. The fiction (or nonfiction) narrative test will emphasize the assessment of word choice according to district notification. You plan a

Table 5.1	National Board Language Arts Standards and the Brain-Compatible Framework
Brain-Compatible Classroom Principles	**NBPTS Core Propositions and Standards for Accomplished Teachers of Early Adolescent/English Language Arts (EA/ELA)**
1. SAFETY. The classroom must be a safe, caring, and trusting environment before learning—beyond that which is necessary for survival—can take place. *2. RESPECT.* Each child is unique with a combination of individual learning styles that, when respected and encouraged, can flourish. *3. NOVELTY.* Interesting, novel, and challenging activities create positive emotional states that increase real learning opportunities. *4. MEMORY.* Existing memories, when tapped into and built upon, influence genuine learning and nourish new life-long memories. **Six Features of Effective Instruction** 1. *Students learn skills* and knowledge in multiple lesson types. 2. *Teachers integrate test preparation* into instruction. 3. *Teachers make connections* across instruction, curriculum, and life. 4. *Students learn strategies* for doing the work. 5. *Students are expected to be generative thinkers.* 6. *Classrooms foster cognitive collaboration.* *Langer, J.A. (2004). Getting to Excellent: How to Create Better Schools. NY: Teachers College Press.*	Teachers 1. are committed to students and their learning; 2. know the subjects they teach and how to teach those subjects to students; 3. are responsible for managing and monitoring student learning; 4. think systematically about their practice and learn from experience; 5. are members of learning communities. **NBPTS Standards for Accomplished Teachers of Early Adolescent/English Language Arts (EA/ELA) with Writing Standard IX (summarized)** IX. Writing Teachers help writers • work on their style and voice; • understand about form and function and the power of word choice; • understand writing is a process of thinking and rethinking, writing and rewriting; • ask students to help create rubrics or other tools for critiquing writing; • discover they have something to say. Teachers • know inexperienced writers exhibit predictable patterns; • know students are motivated to write when ideas have meaning in their lives; • assist students in reflecting on their writing; • provide exemplary models and suggest strategies; • respond to student writing as trusted adults first and foremost; • pair students to read and orally retell each other's work to determine how successfully it communicates; • encourage students writing efforts as a means of enjoyment but also as a valuable lifelong skill. I. Knowledge of Students X. Language Study II. Knowledge of the Field XI. Integrated III. Engagement Instruction IV. Learning Environment XII. Assessment V. Equity, Fairness, Diversity XII. Self-Reflection VI. Instructional Resources XIV. Professional VII. Instructional Decision Making Community VIII. Reading XV. Family IX. Listening, Speaking, Outreach Viewing *Download information on the P standards for your certificated area and learn more about the certification process by visiting NBPTS Web site at www.nbpts.org.

three-day lesson aimed at helping students learn strategies to write more effectively. Experience tells you most of your students' writing exhibits marginal proficiency with respect to word choice. You believe that by helping students discover the power of exact language, you will help increase their personal satisfaction with their writing as well as with their writing-test scores.

The activities you plan rely on brain-friendly pedagogy to keep students safe and stimulated rather than bothered or bored. The novelty of the activities you plan challenge students to think about word choice in new and interesting ways. Students complete a warm-up that involves mystery-oriented sentences. After reading the sentences, they must identify which were better, explain why they were better, and identify any words that made the sentences better.

A discussion of a movie clip shown without sound elicits initial student thoughts on the power of word choice. For instance, the opening scene from *The Fog* (Carpenter, 1978) shows wide-eyed, obviously frightened boy scouts listening to an old sea captain recounting a scary story. You might ask students to think about what the man might be saying to elicit such frightened faces. Encourage them to describe, paint word pictures, and use details. As your students share their answers, you write the criteria they identify for powerful word choice at the top of the grab bag (see Chapters 3 and 5) you draw on the board. (You use grab bags instead of traditional word lists regularly to add visual interest to your instructional tools.)

To help students maintain their focus on the goal, you continually share goals and expectations with students via PowerPoint, overheads, and whiteboard cues. You compliment students during your discussions of word choice, honoring the connections they make and letting them know they indeed have something important to say. Reminding your students that learning is both fun and hard work, you reflect your research-based understanding of the brain's curiosity and its need for safety and stimulation.

Your knowledge of how early adolescents learn and of the importance of novelty and engagement is reflected in your resources and activities: for example, playing mystery music as students enter the classroom each day or playing a version of the Clue game to sustain interest and curiosity. Preparing vague sentences (e.g., "Someone heard something.") reflects your knowledge of the predictable word-choice patterns exhibited by inexperienced writers who, when given the opportunity, learn how to improve, as illustrated with one student's sentence: "Branches scratched the window

> It isn't enough for students to be in a stimulating environment—they have to help create it and directly interact with it. They have to have many opportunities to tell their stories, not just listen to the teacher's stories.
>
> —Robert Sylwester

pane." Grab bags you draw on your whiteboard are soon filled with exact verbs, nouns, and adjectives your students offer. Your grab-bag strategy is helping students appreciate the power of word choice they are discovering.

Open-ended questions to students easily satisfied with first efforts illustrate the respectful feedback you offer that helps such students rethink their predictable word choice and rework their sentences. Activities and reinforcing statements to students whom you call your "budding writers" encourage them to understand writing is a process of thinking, rethinking, writing, and revising. Because you embrace the brain-compatible principle of respect, you find it easy to avoid laughing when a student writes, "I heard shrieks coming

from a kitchen door." Without guile you ask guiding questions: "Did you mean to give life to your door like in a Harry Potter story?" and the student realizes she meant to write "*from behind* the door."

Reading activities completed in the computer lab on the second day demonstrate your systematic thinking about available technology that will help support your goals. Prescreened for their appropriateness, you direct students to a variety of Internet sites with readings that appeal to various ability levels and interests. Links to student mystery writers from districts across the country, urban legends from the Southeast and Mexico, and a middle school adaptation of Poe's "The Fall of the House of Usher" offer your students a variety of purposeful and diverse reading opportunities. While in the lab, students compile (in grab bag handouts) exact words from their readings, words that appeal to them, help create mood, and can possibly be useful to their own writing. The uniformity of your handout's grab bag to classroom grab bags is important. Maintaining continuity between class work and lab work helps students think systematically about achieving their goal to become stronger writers.

Reading to write better! Let's see how writers do it. Read the following excerpt. Underline words that grab your attention and create the atmosphere of mystery we have been exploring.

"The Fall of the House of Usher"*
By Edgar Allan Poe

At last I came into view of the lonely house of Usher. The day had been dark and dreary, and the long horseback ride over a _____ desolate section of English countryside had mead me tired and depressed.

It was almost dark when I first saw the house. Its ancient walls and vacant eyelike windows looked decayed and dying.

It was a stone structure, two stories in height, that stood at the very edge of a dark lake whose waters splashed and beat at the foundation. Patches of green moss climbed the walls in several places as if trying to hide the cracks in the mortar that held the stones together. In some places the stones themselves were cracked and crumbling.

As you continue today's readings, pay attention to the exact words and phrases that "grab" you and add them to your grab bag.

---

*Excerpt from abridged version of "The Fall of the House of Usher" by E. A. Poe. *Stories From Four Corners.* (Amsco Publishers), pp.48-59.

Name _____

FROM VAGUE TO EXACT WRITING!

Written Practice

Use the underlined words in these vague sentences to create sentences that are more exact and interesting.

1. It was a <u>windy</u> night. *The wind howled throughout the darkened forest.*

2. It was <u>rainy</u> out. *The rain* _____

_____

_____

3. It was <u>snowy</u> out. _____

_____

_____

4. It was <u>thunder</u>ing out. _____

_____

_____

5. There was a full <u>moon</u>. _____

_____

_____

If you finish early, use the back of your paper to brainstorm ideas for a mystery story you might like to write. Think about words that will grab your audience's attention the same way the scout master grabbed the attention of the boys seated around the campfire in the scene we watched earlier.

- Where might the story take place?
- Who might your main character be?
- What exact words and phrases might you include in the opening of your story?

WRITE ON!

Name *Jeff*

From Vague to EXACT *Writing!*

OPENING PARAGRAPH OF MY EXACT— NOT VAGUE—MYSTERY STORY

- Remember to use precise and exact words.
- Don't summarize your story. Produce the images of your story!
- Do not reveal what happens too soon! Leave your readers wanting more!

The clouds slowly rolled away form the moon that revealed its bright light. The wind whistled in the trees. A spine-chilling how came out of the forest sending the night critters scampering to their shelters.

- **Do not write** more than two paragraphs.
- Review your exact word grab bags
- Remember the importance of exact word choice to create the atmosphere in your opening.

You invite students to apply all they have learned about word choice to writing the opening paragraph of a mystery. Your three-day lesson has promoted learning for all your students, including those usually frustrated who willingly revised their work after peer conferencing helped them learn the strategies to do the work.

You groomed your students for success throughout the three-day lesson. All the activities you planned helped students learn the strategies to do the work of grabbing audience attention through word choice. Remaining on the board is the simple rubric for word choice you and your students developed on the first day. You set on your resource table exemplary student samples from previous years to serve as models. To ensure the success of all your students, you provide a modified writing activity for students not comfortable with or interested in writing a mystery paragraph. Such students will choose words from any grab bag to write discrete, exact sentences that demonstrate their word choice prowess.

By the third day reading, writing, listening, speaking, and viewing activities have helped your students understand and apply the power of word choice. When you ask students to reflect on the payoff writers get from using effective word choice, one student answers, "Word choice keeps readers reading instead of putting them to sleep." The answer, as well as the paragraphs and sentences your students have written, reinforce the success of your lesson on word choice. You are satisfied but not surprised when your students' scores on the district assessment test are strong, particularly in the category of word choice.

Satisfied, you reflect on novelty, the brain-compatible principle related to student engagement that inspired the lesson that helped students learn the strategies to do the work. You are convinced: lessons that are both challenging and fun foster the learning derived from working within the brain-compatible framework for student achievement.

SETTING THE STAGE FOR AUTHENTIC ASSESSMENT AND LEARNING

As brain-compatible teachers, we must hold our students to high, challenging standards while at the same time encouraging their participation. Showing students how to be successful and providing them with assessment tools that are user-friendly and sensitive to their diverse backgrounds is essential. After all, assessment tools, to be fair, must be understandable and usable by all. Whether teachers develop charts themselves or acquire them from colleagues or the Internet, charts must be useful to their particular groups of students.

While serving as a facilitator of writing and rubrics learning communities, I was committed to explaining the value of using rubrics as an instructional tool. Suggestions I would like to share from my experience as an NBCT and facilitator of learning communities include the following:

- Evaluate and modify assessment tools you develop or download from the Internet. Any rubric chart, including the ones I provide in this chapter, have little value if they are not clear to all your students.

- When designing rubric charts, whether alone or with students, place the rubrics (e.g., word choice) in the stub (i.e., initial left-hand) column so that students clearly see the specific traits being assessed.

- Maintain a supply of student writing and project samples (or prepare some yourselves) that serve as models for students. Show students what it takes to achieve.

- Share with students the standards and curricular objectives that guide your decision making so they have a deeper understanding of their learning journey.

Showcasing the Work Our Students Do

Portfolios are an effective way to archive student assignments and document their progress. Portfolios provide an organizational tool that allows students to monitor their own progress and share their work with teachers, peers, parents, or guardians. Portfolios give students a historical base from which to appreciate their own progress over the course of a term or year. They are important because they provide an orderly mechanism for teachers to evaluate students in an ongoing way.

PAMELA'S STORY

Pamela is a middle and high school counselor who works with English language learners and special needs students who have not passed high-stakes tests in reading and writing. When asked to evaluate the merit of a rubric chart I had brought to a meeting, she wasted no time in identifying many words that she knew would have little or no meaning for the students she was helping. The words she highlighted included *coherence, disjointed, monotonous, awkward, rambling, obscured meaning, shortcomings, engaging, expressive.*

Pamela respected her students' learning needs. She realized that to help students learn strategies to succeed on future tests, she needed to first make them feel safe. That meant revising the chart with her students' help, using words they understood, while at the same time helping them learn the words that confused them so they would ultimately understand how they were being scored.

Her efforts are representative of the learning acquired by all learning community members who ultimately come to appreciate that teachers must take ownership of the assessment tools we use to grade our students. When we put in the effort to study the intent of rubrics, we realize they are instructional tools that serve as guideposts. Some of us use rubrics because we believe in them. Others use rubrics because states have mandated their use (and in so doing, compromised the integrity of rubrics as instructional tools). Regardless, the guiding language imbedded in rubrics ultimately serves to help us help our students learn the strategies to do the work.

Self-evaluation instruments are also integral to the portfolio. They encourage learners to reflect on their growth as writers, connecting the memories of who they *were* as writers to the writers they have become.

Scoring the Work Our Students Do

Writing about assessment and the learning brain, Ronis (2006) defined a rubric as "an established set of criteria used for scoring or rating students' tests, portfolios, or performances" (p. 80). The two types of rubric scoring that states use to score high-stakes writing tests are holistic and analytic. Holistic scoring evaluates the overall impression presented by a student's work. By contrast, analytic scoring provides separate scores for different traits, such as word choice, one of six writing traits in the writing rubric (which appears later in the chapter). Analytic scoring is more detailed than holistic, thereby providing more information to you and your students. Critics (e.g., Nitko, 2004) rightfully have noted that both analytic and holistic scoring can be subjective. This is especially true when teachers are poorly trained, do not receive the ongoing training necessary to ensure interrater reliability, or do not believe in rubrics in the first place.

Many writing teachers feel district- and state-mandated writing-rubric systems represent outside interference. Yes, the challenge is formidable, especially when some districts offer participation in intensive training workshops, whereas others secure volumes of information on rubrics, expecting their teachers to decipher and implement the assessment tools independent of meaningful training. Our brains tend to balk at such coercion and indifference. Anger and frustration often follow our resistance, especially when we don't understand or necessarily agree with mandated interventions.

> Elementary teachers often ask their students to reflect on their performance using simpler language.
>
> I put a period at the end of my sentence. ☺ ☺ ☹

Even though rubrics have become ersatz scorecards of the high-stakes testing machine, they remain an invaluable instructional tool for helping students learn the strategies of effective writing. Although no system is completely objective, with diligent and ongoing training (or self-directed learning), an assessment system based on rubrics comes close.

Scoring Value of Rubrics

Table 5.2 illustrates how 6-point scores convert to letter and percent values. It is important to share this information with students, who may assume fractional equivalents. While 4/6 in rubric terms demonstrates proficiency, its fractional equivalent is 66 percent! Help students understand the difference. You may need to modify the conversions to match your school's rating system or to include more subtle increments, for example, 4+ = B+ = 85–89.

Helping Students Learn the Strategies to Assess

The best way to get students engaged in their own learning is to have them evaluate their work and the work of their peers. Rubrics offer a brain-compatible tool for guiding learners through the self-assessment processes, ultimately helping them to become critical thinkers, realistic self-assessors, and proficient writers.

Everyone benefits from rubrics, especially students who enjoy opportunities to play "teacher" whether scoring their own work or that of their peers. The Learning Pyramid (see Chapter 7) suggests that students retain 70 percent of what they learn when they practice as they learn and 90 percent of

Table 5.2	Rubric Score Conversions	
Rubric Score	**Letter**	**Percent**
6	A+	96–100
5	A	90–95
4	B	80–89
3	C	70–79
2	D	65–69
1	F	64 or less

what they learn when they teach others. When students use rubrics to assess the work of their peers, they build neural connections of learning through their very conversations. They not only benefit from being exposed to the language and criteria of rubrics but also benefit from learning how to self-administer feedback through each stage of the writing process. Reaching their instructional goals is so much easier for our students when we help them learn the strategies to do the work!

I always ask students to self-assess major writing assignments before turning in final copies and to score their work using the writing-rubric chart. For each of the six writing traits, students circle the statement they believe describes their performance. By asking learners to justify their responses, I learn whether they are authentically using the charts or merely going through the motions. For example, a student may circle a 4 for word choice. "I think I earned a 4 because I tried really hard" is not an effective justification and would prompt me to have a conference with the student to check his under-standing of justifying scores as well as his understanding of each rubric.

I have students staple their circled rubric score sheet (which is reduced to a half sheet to conserve paper) to their work. I use a yellow highlighter to denote my scores. As the year progresses, I find myself highlighting over student-drawn circles indicating proficiency more often, suggesting students are not only learning the strategies to write and write well but also becoming more proficient at *knowing* they are proficient.

Setting the Stage for Constructive Feedback

Helping students learn the strategies of effective peer conferencing engages students thoroughly. Locate a weak writing sample, such as the one following, and use the sample to teach appropriate conferencing-feedback techniques.

AUTUMN

The trees' look nice they are pretty. I like to walk threw the leaves, sometimes its windy. Then my friends and me go roller-blading. Roller-blading is cool my friends think their better than me no way! I'm the best. The other day I jumped over a gigantic ramp.

Place a copy of the writing sample on your document camera or overhead (or you can prepare and distribute copies). Explain to the students the sample represents the opening paragraph of a descriptive piece about autumn. Ask for a volunteer with a thick skin to pretend the piece is hers. Direct the learner to read the piece aloud and ask you: "Will you be my conference partner?" Now the fun begins. Have the volunteer ask you to answer the following questions:

What's the strongest part in my work?
What's the weakest part in my work?
Does my work have a clear purpose and direction?
Do you have any questions about my work?
Do you have any suggestions about my work?

For the first interaction, be unmerciful: *"There is no strong part. . . . The weakest part? How do I choose? It's totally weak! . . . There is no purpose! . . . Why did you write it is the question I have! . . . Dump it is my only suggestion."*

After you are done with your verbal lashing, ask the class: "How'd I do? Was I an effective conferencing partner?" Trust me. Kids know. They will most assuredly let you know you were very mean and unkind, not at all helpful to your writing partner.

For the second interaction, be too polite but vague as you respond to the questions: *"It was all strong. . . . No weak parts. . . . Sure, it has a clear purpose. . . . I have no questions. . . . I have no suggestions other than writing it neater so the teacher sees a first draft—you know how teachers are."*

Once again, ask the class to comment. Once again, they will let you know you were too nice and you were not being honest.

Ask students what you should have said and how you should have said it. What follows, of course, are responses that demonstrate polite and constructive feedback responses that produce effective revision suggestions for a writer to consider.

- "Walking through the leaves" creates a pleasurable visual image of autumn. I wanted to hear more about that. Is there more you could share with the reader about this experience? Remember the 5-Ws: Who, What, When, Where, Why. The more details you can provide, the more the readers will feel like they're walking through the leaves with you.
- When the mood shifts suddenly from walking through the leaves on a windy day to roller-blading, I feel ripped off. I want to know more about autumn and what that means to you. Is there more you might tell the reader about your walk in the leaves?
- Although the words "threw" and "through" are pronounced the same, they have different meanings. Let's define them and see which one fits this context.
- When you read aloud what you wrote, are there places where a pause is natural? What punctuation marks tell the reader it's time to pause? Do you have them in place? Let's read the piece together and see.
- Did you proofread your work when you were done writing it? Were there words that you weren't sure how to spell? Let's review your piece and use the dictionary to help us correct words that may not be spelled how they sound.

Help Yourself, Help Others

By encouraging students to use the following list of questions when they conference with peers, you help them learn the important art of constructive criticism, essential to sustaining a safe and respectful workshop environment. As they repeat the process of peer conferencing, students come to appreciate the intent and value of using scripted questions. At some point they no longer need the list of questions that follows, because they have learned the strategy.

*What do you like **best** about the work?*
*What do you like **least** about the work?*
Does the work contain unnecessary details or information?
*Does the work have **too much** information?*
*What **questions** do you have after carefully reading the work?*
*What **suggestions** do you have after carefully reading this work?*

AUTUMN DAY SAMPLER

Use the following opening paragraphs from the "An Autumn Day" assignment to learn the strategy of conference etiquette and how to evaluate writing using the writing rubrics chart found in this chapter.

SAMPLE 1

One day I walked through the woods. I noticed the trees were very pretty. The colors of the leaves were beginning to turn. I like when that happens. They were gold and orange and red. The air was cool I could smell something burning.

SAMPLE 2

The trees' look nice they are pretty. I like to walk threw the leaves, sometimes its windy. Then my friends and me go roller-blading. Roller-blading is cool my friends think their better than me no way! I'm the best. The other day I jumped over a gigantic ramp.

SAMPLE 3

I heard footsteps crunch in the fallen leaves. A squirrel ran out to greet me. The air was cool and crisp. The leaves were golden and moving in the autumn breeze. I love autumn! I love the chill that makes me button my sweater as I stroll through the forest.

Rubrics and Assessment Sampler

Look at the sample charts included in this chapter and compare them with the evaluation requirements of your school or district. Revise them to suit your needs and the needs of your students. I use different colored paper to distinguish the various rubrics and assessments for ease of identification inside student portfolios.

The rubrics charts and assessments that follow will, I hope, inspire you to use them or develop new ones. When used regularly, rubrics and assessment tools help students understand more fully the standards by which they are scored.

Rubric 5.1 Writing

	6 Superior — Exceeds expectations.	5 Strong — Shows control and skill. Many strengths evident.	4 Maturing — Strengths outweigh weaknesses.	3 Developing — Strengths and weaknesses are about equal. First draft effect.	2 Emerging — Isolated moments of ability. Shortcomings dominate.	1 Struggling — Isolated moments of ability. Shortcomings dominate.
Idea and Content	Exceptionally clear, focused, and interesting.	Clear, focused, and interesting.	Clear and focused.	Overly general. Predictable. Occasionally off topic.	Somewhat unclear. Minimal development.	Lack of central idea. Minimal development or unclear.
Organization of Thoughts	Consistently strong, effective sequencing.	Strong, effective sequencing.	Sequencing clear. May be formulaic.	Inconsistent, undeveloped, obvious.	Lacking consistency or coherence.	Lacking coherence, disjointed.
Word Choice	Exceptionally precise, interesting.	Precise, interesting.	Functional, appropriate.	Ordinary. lacking, precision	Monotonous and/ or misused.	Extremely limited. Vague, imprecise.
Sentence Fluency	Consistently strong, varied, expressive.	Strong, varied.	Somewhat varied.	Occasionally awkward. Limited variety.	Awkward, rambling.	Incomplete. Rambling, awkward. Obscured meaning.
Voice	Exceptionally expressive, engaging.	Expressive, engaging.	Occasionally expressive, engaging.	Inappropriately personal or impersonal with audience.	Mostly flat or overly personal or impersonal with audience.	Flat. No sense of audience awareness.
Conventions and Mechanics	Very few errors/ barely noticeable.	Few errors.	Minor errors do not impede readability.	Limited control. Errors begin to impede readability.	Little control. Frequent errors impede readability.	Numerous errors impede readability. Need for extensive editing.

What do you like **best** about the work?
What do you like **least** about the work?
Does the work contain unnecessary details or information?
Does the work have **too much** information?

What **questions** do you have after carefully reading the work?
What **suggestions** do you have after carefully reading this work?

Used in conjunction with the Writing Rubrics' bookmark, students have a clear direction to more effective writing

Rubric 5.2 Writing Rubric Bookmark

Six Traits of Good Writing
and Their Rubrics

IDEAS AND CONTENT
- narrow topic
- fresh original ideas
- relevant quality details
- accurate supportive details

ORGANIZATION
- inviting introduction
- thoughtful transitions
- logical and effective sequencing
- controlled pacing
- smooth and balanced overall effect
- satisfying conclusion

VOICE
- strong interaction between reader and writer
- appropriate for the purpose and the audience
- reflects strong commitment to topic

WORD CHOICE
- specific and accurate
- creates pictures
- effective verbs, nouns, etc.
- precise use of words
- clichés and jargon used sparingly

SENTENCE FLUENCY
- well-constructed sentences
- strong, varied and purposeful sentence structure and length
- natural dialogue (if applicable)
- fragments, *if used,* add style

CONVENTIONS AND MECHANICS
- correct spelling, grammar, usage, format, etc.
- control of capitalization, punctuation, etc.

Scoring Guide Criteria

6/Superior
Exceeds expectations.

5/Strong
Shows control and skill. Many strengths evident.

4/Maturing/Proficient
Strengths outweigh weaknesses.

3/Developing
Strengths and weaknesses are about equal. First draft effect.

2/Emerging
Isolated moments of ability. Shortcomings dominate.

1/Struggling
Results are lacking.
Writer needs assistance.

Notes
- This abbreviated scoring guide is based on a 6-trait system currently used to score many state writing tests as well as the National Assessment for Educational Progress (NAEP) writing assessments.

- These criteria can be used to assess each rubric, providing students a clear sense of where they are and where they need to be as writers.

- Learn your state's rubric and scoring system! Use of rubrics and criteria may be the single most effective way to empower students with a real understanding of what proficient and superior writing looks like.

- Invite students to write their names on the back of the bookmark before laminating. Add contact information, classroom rules, whatever you wish!

Rubric 5.3 Reading Rubrics' Criteria Chart

	6 Superior	5 Strong	4 Proficient	3 Developing	2 Emerging	1 Struggling
Response	Sophisticated, thorough, perceptive.	Complex.	Satisfactory.	Less than satisfactory.	Random, somewhat unclear.	Unclear. Incomplete or inappropriate.
Understanding of Text	Extremely thorough.	Thorough.	Somewhat complete.	Limited evidence.	Very limited evidence.	Little or no evidence.
Extension of Text	Insightful and considerable.	Considerable.	Appropriate but may be minimal.	Incomplete.	Incomplete with lack of accuracy or focus.	Inaccurate and/ or incomplete, irrelevant, incoherent.
Evaluation and Appreciation of Textual Ideas and Features	Extensive.	Thorough.	Adequate.	Minimal.	Somewhat unclear or inaccurate.	None or illogical, unclear, unsatisfactory.

Response
Appropriate to purpose
Relevant quality details
Supportive details
and ideas

Understanding of Text
Consider multiple interpretations
Draw inference from textual cues
Differentiate between literal and figurative
Attend to/explore ambiguities and contradictions.

Extension of Text
Make connection to life, other works, ideas
Use text to generate, validate, reflect

Evaluation and Appreciation of Textual Ideas and Features
Questioning
Critiquing, agreeing, disagreeing
Speculating

Rubric 5.4 Reading Response With Four Scoring Values

	4 Strong	3 Proficient	2 Maturing	1 Struggling
Response Appropriate to purpose Relevant, quality details Supportive details and ideas	Sophisticated, thorough, perceptive.	Satisfactory.	Random, somewhat unclear.	Unclear Incomplete or inappropriate.
Understanding of Text Considers multiple interpretations Draw inference from textual cues Differentiate between literal and figurative Attend to/explore ambiguities and contradictions	Extremely thorough.	Somewhat complete.	Very limited evidence.	Little or no evidence.
Extension of Text Make connection to life, other works, ideas Use text to generate, validate, reflect	Insightful and considerable.	Appropriate but may be minimal.	Incomplete with lack of accuracy or focus.	Inaccurate and/or incomplete, irrelevant, incoherent.
Evaluation and Appreciation of Textual Ideas and Features Questioning Critiquing, agreeing, disagreeing Speculating	Extensive.	Adequate.	Somewhat unclear or inaccurate.	No response or response is severely lacking or unclear.

Rubric 5.5 Group Work

	6 Superior Exceeds expectations.	5 Strong Shows control and skill. Many strengths evident.	4 Maturing Strengths outweigh weakness.	3 Developing Strengths and weak-ness are about equal. First draft effect.	2 Emerging Isolated moments of ability. Shortcomings dominate.	1 Struggling Results are lacking. Writer needs assistance.
Cooperation and Participation	Exceptional equity of sharing workload.	Excellent equity of sharing workload.	Evidence of sharing workload.	Sharing work apparent most of the time.	Inequitable unfair distribution of work.	Unreasonable distribution of work. Intervention required.
Task Organization and Planning	Effective/logical sequencing of task objectives.	Logical sequencing of task objectives.	Sequencing of task objectives attempted.	Sequencing of tasks attempted though gaps occur.	Efforts seem random and without order.	Random attempts to organize group. Requires intervention.
Attention to Task	Exceptional and clear enthusiasm and effort.	Clear enthusiasm and effort.	Effort is evident.	Sometimes distractions divert attention.	Distractions divert attention.	Numerous off-task distractions. Requires intervention.
Quiet Voices	Consistent clear evidence.	Clear evidence.	Evidence.	Sometimes members distract others.	Members often distract others.	Inappropriate noise. Requires intervention.
Completion of Task	Exceptional completion with insightful additions or variations.	Fully completed with few editions.	Completed.	Basically completed.	Lacks completion.	Incomplete, poorly done.

Group Names/Overall Score

Name _____ /_____ Name _____ /_____

Name _____ /_____ Name _____ /_____

Note: Sometimes it is clear that one or two members of a group are not doing their fair share. Should you observe this common situation, remind the students to be honest when they discuss within their groups what their scores should be. Class discussions on the challenges and fairness of group work and ensuring grades encourages more individual responsibility within the group. Have a group leader record the first day's score. Then, rather than distribute a new sheet for the next group session, have students note their performance using arrows next to or above their names and score. ↑ for better; → for about the same; ↓ worse than the previous day's effort. You will be impressed at the honesty your groups of students use to evaluate their own and each others' performance.

Rubric 5.6 Oral Presentation

	6 Superior Exceeds expectations.	5 Strong Shows control and skill. Many strengths evident.	4 Maturing Strengths outweigh weaknesses.	3 Developing Strengths and weaknesses are about equal.	2 Emerging Isolated moments of ability. Shortcomings dominate.	1 Struggling Results are lacking. Speaker needs assistance.
Presentation of Topic Addressed	Compelling, clear and focused.	Clear and focused.	Clear.	Overly general or simplistic at times.	Unclear or minimal.	Lacks any central or clear idea.
Organization of Thoughts	Exceptionally clear sequencing.	Effective sequencing.	Clear sequencing though may be simplistic.	Inconsistent or confusing.	Randomness or incoherence dominates.	Lacking any logic or coherence of thought.
Poise With Attention to Audience • Eye Contact • Vocal Expression	Exceptional.	Effective.	Adequate.	Adequate with some lapses.	Little attention to connection with and obligation to audience.	No attention to connection with and obligation to audience.
Accurate • Examples • Details • Description	Extremely effective with strong correlation to topic.	Strong correlation to topic.	Good correlation to topic. Some less useful than others.	Adequate with some details incorrect or irrelevant.	Incorrect or irrelevant examples, details, etc.	Seriously incorrect or irrelevant examples, details, etc.
Preparation and Appropriate Use of Visual Aids	Exceptional.	Effective.	Adequate.	Some aspects may be obvious or irrelevant.	Visual aids mostly trite or irrelevant.	Visual aids severely trite or irrelevant.

Name _____   Score _____

Rubric 5.7 Debate

	6 Superior Exceeds expectations.	5 Strong Shows control and skill. Many strengths evident.	4 Proficient Strengths outweigh weaknesses.	3 Developing Strengths and weaknesses are about equal.	2 Emerging Isolated moments of ability. Shortcomings dominate.	1 Struggling Results are lacking. Student needs assistance.
Member/s Attention to Appearance	All members exceptionally well groomed.	Majority of members well groomed.	All members appropriately groomed.	Most members groomed appropriately.	Few members groomed appropriately.	Lacking evidence appropriately groomed.
Logic of Argument	Exceptionally compelling and clear sequencing of argument.	Clear sequencing of argument.	Clear, though may be occasionally obvious or simplistic.	Inconsistent. Occasionally confusing.	Random or faulty logic dominates.	Lacking any logic or coherence of thought.
Use of Sources, Statistics and Other Data	Extremely effective with strong correlation to main argument.	Effective.	Adequate. Some date may be less useful than others.	Some data is irrelevant or incorrect.	Irrelevant, trite, or inaccurate.	None evident or seriously incorrect or irrelevant.
Use of Charts or Other Displays	Exceptionally effective and relevant.	Effective and relevant.	Adequate.	Some displays may be obvious or irrelevant.	Displays and their use are somewhat irrelevant or trite.	Severely lacking or irrelevant or none.
Opening Statement and Rebuttal	Compelling, clear, and focused.	Clear and focused.	Clear.	Occasionally overly general or simplistic.	Unclear or minimal.	Lacks a central or clear idea.

Total Score _____ /36

Rubric 5.8 Multimedia

	6 Superior Exceeds expectations.	5 Strong Shows control and skill. Many strengths evident.	4 Maturing Strengths outweigh weaknesses.	3 Developing Strengths and weaknesses are about equal.	2 Emerging Isolated moments of ability. Shortcomings dominate.	1 Struggling Results are lacking. Student needs assistance.
Idea and Content Text Graphics Number of slides	Exceptional. Multiple text, graphics, slides (including links) support objective in a superior way.	Majority of text, graphics, slides support objective.	More than half text, graphics, slides support objective.	At least half text, graphics, slides support objective.	Little evidence that text, graphics, slides support objective.	Lacking evidence that text, graphics, slides support objective.
Organization Slides/Layout Clarity Timing	Exceptional evidence of attention to presenting information clearly and logically.	Strong evidence of attention to presenting information clearly and logically.	Good evidence of attention to presenting information clearly and logically.	Adequate evidence, with minor inconsistencies or flaws.	Randomness or incoherence dominates.	Lacking any logic or coherence.
Style *with respect to* Word Choice Sentence Fluency Voice	Exceptionally precise and interesting. Extremely engaging.	Strong, Interesting and engaging.	Functional and appropriate. Occasionally engaging.	Occasionally awkward or lacking precision and/or engagement.	Monotonous. Awkward. Flat, with little engagement.	Imprecise, rambling, or obscured meaning. Flat, with no sense of audience.
Conventions and Mechanics Spelling, capitalization, punctuation, etc. Legibility: text size, font, contrast	Very few errors. Barely noticeable.	Few errors.	Minor errors do not impede readability.	Limited control. Errors begin to impede readability.	Little control. Frequent and significant errors impede readability.	Numerous errors seriously impede readability. Need for extensive editing.

Total Score _____ /36

Rubric 5.9 Web Page

	6 Superior Exceeds expectations.	5 Strong Shows control and skill. Many strengths evident.	4 Maturing Strengths outweigh weaknesses.	3 Developing Strengths and weaknesses are about equal.	2 Emerging Isolated moments of ability. Shortcomings dominate.	1 Struggling Results are lacking.
Idea and Content Text Graphics Number of pages Links	Exceptional. Multiple text, graphics, pages, links support objective in a superior way.	Majority of text, graphics, pages, links support objective.	More than half text, graphics, pages, and links (if used) support objective.	At least half text, graphics, pages, links (if used) support objective.	Little evidence that text, graphics, pages, links (if used) support objective.	Lacking evidence that text, graphics, pages support objective.
Organization Page/s Layout Navigation	Exceptional evidence of attention to layout of information, making navigation very clear and logical.	Strong evidence. of attention to layout of information, making navigation clear and logical.	Good evidence of attention to layout of information. Navigation clear most of the time.	Adequate evidence with minor inconsistencies or flaws.	Randomness or incoherence dominates.	Lacking any logic or coherence.
Style Word choice Sentence fluency Voice	Exceptionally precise and interesting. Extremely engaging.	Strong, Interesting and engaging.	Functional and appropriate. Occasionally engaging.	Occasionally awkward or lacking precision and/or engagement.	Monotonous. Awkward. Flat, with little engagement.	Imprecise. Rambling or obscured meaning. Flat, with no sense of audience.
Mechanics Spelling, capitalization, punctuation, etc. Legibility: text size, type, contrast	Very few errors. Barely noticeable.	Few errors.	Minor errors do not impede readability or navigability.	Limited control. Errors begin to impede readability.	Little control. Frequent and significant errors impede readability.	Numerous errors seriously impede readability. Need for extensive editing.

Total Score ____ / 36

RUBRIC SCORE VALUES 🖉

RUBRIC SCORE	PERCENT	LETTER GRADE
6	96–100	A+
5+	95	A
5	90	A-
4+	85	B+
4	80	B
3+	75	C+
3	70	C
2+	65	D+
2	60	D
1	59 or less	F

Help Yourself—Help Others

🖉 **What do you like best about the work?**

🖉 **What do you like least about the work?**

🖉 **Does the work contain unnecessary details or information?**

🖉 **Does the work have too much information?**

🖉 **What questions do you have after carefully reading the work?**

🖉 **What suggestions do you have after carefully reading this work?**

Teacher Tip

Copy rubric score values (above, in Table 5.2, or your own) plus guiding questions such as those you've just read onto the back of rubric charts so that your students have immediate access to important information.

PEER CONFERENCE WORKSHEET
For Exposition or Persuasion

Writer's Name: _____

Conference Partner's Name: _____

Directions for Conference Partners

1. Read the writer's work carefully and evaluate it, using the check list below.
2. Next to each, write *Yes, No,* or *Needs improvement.* Explain your answers to your partner.
3. If you have been given permission to conference orally, use this worksheet to guide your conference.

Content

Addresses Prompt? _____
Organization? _____
Effective Support? _____
Clarity of Language? _____
Satisfying Conclusion? _____

Conventions and Mechanics

1. <u>Reread</u> the work carefully. <u>Underline</u> words you are certain your partner did not spell, use (e.g., there, their, they're), or capitalize correctly.
2. <u>Underline</u> words/phrases that are confusing or awkward in any way.

Compliments/Comments

Let your writing partner know what they did well and what needs improvement.

Directions for Writers

Circle the appropriate responses:

I agree with my partner's assessment of my work. Yes   No

I plan on revising and editing my work. Yes   No, I am satisfied with the overall quality of my work.

Additional comment (optional): _____

_____

_____

SELF-REFLECTION. Designed by a high school counselor and student, was used for student self reflection based on weekly sessions with her counselor.

Eloisa's Personal Growth Rubrics	4	3	2	1	Eloisa's Scores
Work towards gaining a better understanding of myself.	I clearly understand what motivates me.	I sort of understand what motivates me.	I think I know what motivates me.	I have no clue what motivates me.	
Important things/ people in my life	I know the five most important things/people in my life.	I know the three important things/people in my life.	I know the two important things/people in my life.	I don't know what is important to me at all.	
Strengths and weaknesses	I have identified my strengths and weaknesses.	I am getting to know my strengths and weaknesses.	I have started to think about my strengths and weaknesses.	I don't know my strengths and weaknesses.	
Improving school attendance	I attend school everyday.	I miss one day or less per week.	I miss more than one day but less than three days per week.	I miss class three or more days per week.	
Arriving on time to class	I am almost never late to class.	I am late to two or less classes each day.	I am late to three or less classes each day.	I am late to more than three classes each day.	
Turning in completed homework	I turn in 75% of the homework I have completed.	I turn in 50% of the homework I have completed.	I turn in 25% of the homework I have completed.	I turn in less than 25% of the homework I have completed.	
Investigating the writing profession	I have identified and researched the writing programs at four universities.	I have identified and researched the writing programs at three universities.	I have identified and researched the writing programs at two universities.	I have not identified or researched any university writing programs.	
Investigating book publishing	I have researched the first four steps to publishing a book.	I have researched the first three steps to publishing a book.	I have researched the first two steps to publishing a book.	I have no clue about publishing a book.	

SELF-ASSESSMENT

Name: _____

Title of Work: _____

Circle one: story   poem   essay   summary   other: _____

Refer to your rubric chart as you self-assess your work.

Ideas and Content: I give myself _____ because_____
_____
_____

Organization: I give myself _____ because_____
_____
_____

Word Choice: I give myself _____ because_____
_____
_____

Sentence Fluency: I give myself _____ because_____
_____
_____

Voice: I give myself: I give myself _____ because_____
_____
_____

Conventions and Mechanics: I give myself _____ because_____
_____
_____

Reflection: Based on your self-assessment, what is your plan of action?
_____
_____

Remember: Writers must be their own harshest critics. *Write on!*

STUDENT SELF-ASSESSMENT AND BEST PRACTICE

Self-assessment tools can help students think more reflectively about their lives and their lives as learners. Moreover, the information gathered from student self-assessments can help you learn which activities engage (or fail to engage) students and guide your preparation of more effective lessons and units.

Sample 1

End of Semester Reflection   Name *(optional)* _____

Choose 4 of the following statements and answer in complete sentences. Your answers may reflect any part of your life, not just our classroom.

- The high point of this quarter/semester was . . .
- The low point of this quarter/semester was. . .
- My quarter/semester would have been better if . . .
- Our writing workshop would be better if . . .
- School would be better if . . .
- Something about my behavior that I like most is . . .
- Something about my behavior that I want to work on is . . .

Sample 2

End of Quarter Reflection   Name *(optional)* _____

Please respond to all of the following questions.

- What was your favorite assignment this quarter and why?
- What personal skills or talents did you use to complete this assignment?
- What knowledge did you gain about yourself or personal strengths did you recognize after having completed this quarter?
- What would you have enjoyed spending more time on and why?
- Our next quarter involves persuasive argument. What topic would you most like to argue for or against (for example, uniforms in public schools)?

QUESTIONS FOR REFLECTION

1. Which brain-compatible principles support the use of rubrics as an important component of an authentic assessment system?

2. What considerations do you make to meet the diverse needs of your students?

3. What do you think it takes to make a good rubric?

4. Why is it important to consider English language learners and special education students when developing rubrics?

5. Why is it important to involve all students in the process of developing rubrics?

6. What discoveries have you made about rubrics and assessment?

7. Regarding the brain-compatible framework for student achievement, how does the feature of effective instruction related to helping students learn the strategies for doing the work harmonize with

   - Brain-Compatible Principles 1–4: safety; respect; novelty; memory?
   - Core Proposition 3: responsibility for managing and monitoring student learning?

6 Expecting Generative Thinking

We shall make pure and faster progress when we devote
ourselves to finding out just what education is and what
conditions have to be satisfied in order that education
may be a reality and not a name or a slogan.
— John Dewey, *Experience and Education*

Feature 5

Students are expected to be generative thinkers.

Students are expected to be generative thinkers, thinkers who move beyond basics to engage in deeper understandings (Langer, 2000). Generative thinking means more than students going through the motions of playing school to learn basic skills. Chapter 6 explores the research-based characteristics of the effective teachers who expected students to be generative thinkers and who were (likely) more than satisfied with their students' performance in their classrooms and on high-stakes tests.

Learning how successful teachers went about the business of stimulating high levels of thinking that fostered authentic learning and successful performance on high-stakes tests is important. Ironically, ever since high-stakes testing mandates took root, teaching at low levels of learning has never been higher. Ravitch (2006), education scholar and long-time proponent of national standards, described and decried the low levels of learning for which high-stakes testing aim:

> In some districts, children are prepared like trained seals, ready to check off the right box on a standardized test, but completely unprepared to read a complex text, understand the historical roots of contemporary problems, or appreciate the arts as a part of their lives. . . . I reject the idea that education can be reduced solely to reading and mathematics. If that is the only definition of success for schools today, then we veer dangerously close to the possibility that we are schooling our children, but not educating them. A full education is one that prepares students not only to pass tests, but also to read, write, think, speak, and participate in society. We seem to be sacrificing the large goals of education to the near-term needs of politicians. (p. 58)

Our exploration of the feature related to generative thinking will consider its harmony within the brain-compatible framework for student achievement with

- Brain-Compatible Principles 3 and 4: novelty; memory;
- Core Propositions 1 and 4: commitment to students and learning; systematic thinking about best practice and learning from experience. (See Figure 6.1.)

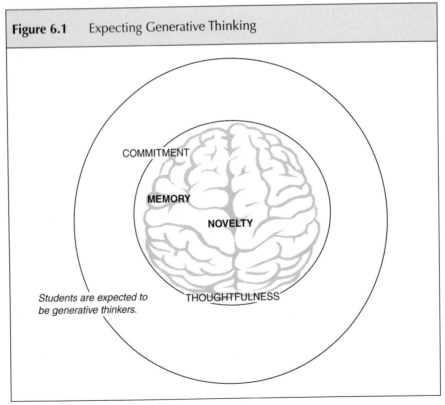

Figure 6.1   Expecting Generative Thinking

COMMITMENT

MEMORY

NOVELTY

Students are expected to be generative thinkers.

THOUGHTFULNESS

CHARACTERISTICS OF FEATURE 5

The effective teachers who expected students to be generative thinkers taught beyond concepts and tests. By contrast teachers whose students did not perform as well typically taught a concept, tested a concept, and moved on to the next concept (Langer, 2000). Effective teachers helped their students to be generative thinkers by designing lessons that asked students higher level thinking questions beyond requirements of basic learning objectives. They engaged students in activities that explored texts from many points of view (e.g., social, historical, ethical, political, personal) and challenged students to write from different points of view and to discuss issues generated by literary texts and students concerns.

Unlike the more successful teachers, typical teachers moved students from one goal to the next. They asked basic questions that satisfied short-term goals but kept students at the low levels of recalling facts instead of continuing their students' thinking and learning processes with questions or activities that encouraged higher levels of thinking and deeper levels of understanding.

In sum, effective teachers were focused on deeper understanding instead of the immediate goals on which typical teachers were focused.

REFLECTING ON THE BRAIN-COMPATIBLE FRAMEWORK AND FEATURE 5

Effective teachers trust their students will be successful and hold them to high standards. They expect their students to be generative thinkers, and they plan activities that make higher-level thinking happen. Intuitively grasping the significance of novelty (Brain-Compatible Principle 3), effective teachers invite students to write letters from different points of view or ask them to create songs and poems based on stories read. By engaging students in interesting or unusual activities, effective teachers stimulate learner interest and foster authentic learning opportunities.

Feature 5 suggests effective teachers focus on deeper understanding to help their students attain higher thinking levels, that is, the analyzing, evaluating, and creating of Bloom's taxonomy. They do not stifle their students' learning by restricting them to the lower levels of remembering, understanding, and applying as do their counterparts who focus on immediate goals. Small wonder the students of effective teachers perform at higher levels on high-stakes tests than do the students of typical teachers. They help students make meaning, make connections that move their learning from working to

A HIGH-STAKES TEACHER'S STORY

"So, what is the setting?" the teacher asks. "Where does the story takes place?"

The third grader enthusiastically replies, "In a fire!"

Troubled by the child's wrong answer (once upon a time, a right answer), the teacher persists: "But where is the fire?"

"In a building, and it's on fire and—!"

"Yes. Okay. But can you tell me the city where the building is on fire?"

The child sighs.

"Can I look back?"

When the teacher nods, the child flips pages to find (finally) the correct answer to the high-stakes reading test question:

"New York."

"Very good."

At last, the teacher relaxes, momentarily hopeful that at least one third grader will earn at least one point on at least one test that may assess knowledge on reading standards related to story setting as defined by time and place.

long-term memory, illustrating how their best practice aligns with Brain-Compatible Principle 4.

Effective teachers understand what typical teachers sometimes do not understand. Higher-level thinking questions are for *all* students. Principals pressured to create (yet) more sections of remedial math, reading, or writing skills should offer counter proposals suggesting the students be placed in classrooms with teachers providing stimulating and thought-provoking learning environments.

Students traditionally destined for remedial test-prep classes have a better chance of succeeding when their brains are rescued from low-level thinking tasks and stimulated by higher level thinking, as suggested by Bloom's seminal work on learning and supported by Pogrow (2006), who described the benefits and success of the twenty-five-year old Higher Order Thinking Skills (HOTS) project. Working to help disadvantaged students become successful, the project dismisses typical routes of test preparation and remediation. Instead, it provides stimulating opportunities that help students learn about learning, for example, through small-group Socratic discussions.

Lessons that nurture higher level thinking require a great deal of time and thoughtful planning that will move students to progressively more complex levels of thinking. As such, effective teachers reflect their harmony with the tenets of NBPTS core propositions related to commitment and thoughtful planning.

Now that you, once again, have seen research on student achievement supporting brain-compatible principles, you are invited to have a look at the brain-compatible framework for high-stakes classrooms in action.

THE BRAIN-COMPATIBLE FRAMEWORK WITH FEATURE 5 IN ACTION

The examples of how teachers expect students to be generative thinkers include my activities as well as those of teachers from elementary, middle, and high school classrooms whom I've had the privilege of observing. (Pseudonyms are used to maintain the teachers' anonymity.) Each teacher consistently motivated students to higher order thinking levels. The students seated in these classrooms were consistently engaged in what can best be described as *learning conversations* with their teachers. Though their objectives differed, each teacher presented learning as a fun experience, which most assuredly helped *engage the whole brain* (Zull, 2004) of each student as each participated in the four learning processes Zull described as getting information, making meaning from it, creating new ideas, and acting on those ideas.

GENERATIVE THINKING IN ELEMENTARY SCHOOL

The two examples that follow are from reading and math classes in a Title I school.

Reading

Rather than assign a lower level thinking activity, fourth-grade teacher Ms. Nans challenged her students to use writing supplies and paper she had precut to create a story element flip book. Instead of having students write the definitions for setting, plot, climax, and other story elements, this effective teacher fostered higher level generative thinking. The students were invited to identify the story elements from any story they had read. For elements like climax, students would really need to *analyze* events carefully to determine accurately which event represented the highest point of excitement in the story.

Ms. Nans showed her care of and interest in student motivation when she responded favorably to their choices: Cinderella? Yes. When a student asked if a Harry Potter story was acceptable, yes was again the reply, but Ms. Nans spent time explaining how subplot climaxes within Potter books might require that the student ask for help, which she promised she would offer. How very different this approach from the teacher in the high-stakes teacher story (earlier in the chapter) who asked narrow questions about setting to the young third grader who so keenly wanted to talk about the plot. Asking about *why* the mommy cat was risking her life to rescue the kittens is one way that teacher could have inspired generative thinking. Can you think of any others?

Math

The class included twenty-seven students: twenty-four second graders, seven of them ELL, and three first graders. Mr. Walsh told his class, "What I want you to do is write a math problem three ways, using numbers, words, and a drawing."

Here are examples of the effective teaching and modeling Mr. Walsh provided to help his students generate thinking:

- He used an overhead projector and poster to show students numbers as words (e.g., 1 → one).
- He provided students with a model he called the *interactive math message* that began with a story about Bob who earned six dimes.
- He asked students thought-provoking questions: for example, "How would you calculate how much six dimes is?" and "What process did you use to get that answer?"
- He invited questions repeatedly: "Who's got questions?"
- He included downtime where he mimed for students to follow basic arm and torso stretches he called *brain gymnastics*. Quietly he said, "Use every ounce of brain power. Concentrate. Let your mind make connections. Remember, your mind, your hands, and your eyes all work together. Now breathe."
- He expressed confidence in his students: "How many of you are a member of the most awesome math class?"

Mr. Walsh planned a lesson that empowered his students to harness higher-level thinking skills necessary to fulfill the formidable objective. Here are some of the examples of the number and word statements and illustrations students produced. (I have maintained their age-appropriate inventive spelling and included the title that one student wrote.)

100 – 60 = 40
I had one dollar. I went to the farm and got some
milk and corn. It cost sixty cence.
I have forty cence left.

● ● ● ● ● ● ● ● ● ● ● ● ● ● ● ● ● ● ● ●

60 + 60 + 60 = 1.80
I went to the store and bought a pot of
flowers. There were three flowers
in each pot. They cost sixty cents each
flower. How much does
each pot cost?

● ● ● ● ● ● ● ● ● ● ● ● ● ● ● ● ● ● ● ●

The Farm
I went to a farm on fryday to clect three dozen eggs.
The price was 50¢ per dozen.
How much did I spend?
3 × 50 = 1.50

● ● ● ● ● ● ● ● ● ● ● ● ● ● ● ● ● ● ● ●

I went to the store and bought
five strawberries I ate two and
then how many did I have left?
Three
5 – 2 = 3

They each cost fifty.
50 + 50 + 50 + 50 + 50 = 2.50

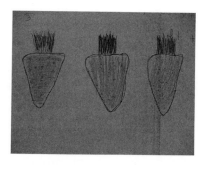

● ● ● ● ● ● ● ● ● ● ● ● ● ● ● ● ● ● ● ●

I have fifteen dogs five of them ran away. I have ten.
15 – 5 = 10

● ● ● ● ● ● ● ● ● ● ● ● ● ● ● ● ● ● ● ●

GENERATIVE THINKING IN MIDDLE SCHOOL

Students are expected to be generative thinkers in middle school too, as the following examples show.

Social Studies

Ms. LaValle stimulated the interest and higher-level thinking of her fifth graders when she developed a summative writing activity on the Constitution. After reading a children's book about the Constitution and its origin to students, Ms. LaValle told the students their job over the next week would involve thinking about what sort of book they would like to write to make the Constitution understandable to middle schoolers. "Just think," she said. "Those guys 200 years ago were not writing for you and me. They were writing for the community back then. The Constitution needed to make sense to them. How will you write a book about the Constitution so it makes sense to your peers today?"

Ms. LaValle told her students she would make available other books besides the one she had already read to them. A discussion followed. She asked students to think about what should be included in the books they would be writing for their middle school audience and to explain why their chosen elements were important to include. She compiled a list on the board as the students generated ideas and support for their ideas. Ms. LaValle told them she would use their ideas to generate the study guide for a unit test they would be taking later on in the unit.

English Immersion

Ms. Crista capitalized on a recent field trip to motivate student interest in an upcoming benchmark test in writing. Her five English language learners engaged in discussion about the field trip comfortably, using the minimal English they had acquired thus far. Four were Hispanic, one Indian. Ms.

Crista guided students through the process of organizing their thoughts by constructing a flow map. Each student completed the map. She provided them down time, which gave the students' working memories necessary processing time.

As the students left the classroom, they each called out a *good-bye phrase*, tapping the phrase they had chosen from an attractively displayed list in the back of the room as they said, "See you later" or "Be right back." Ms. Crista enthusiastically repeated the phrase each learner said. Upon their return, the students tapped a *greeting* as they said it brightly: "Hello" and "What's up?" Again, the teacher replied in kind, adding, "Welcome back to class."

By the end of the day, each student had completed a flow map. The next day they worked on and completed a paragraph about their favorite parts of the field trip experience.

Ms. Crista helped her students reach the highest levels of Bloom's taxonomy, creating a piece of writing. She helped ensure the success of her English language learners by spending time early in the year to ensure a safe and positive learning environment provided in part by her greeting-wall ritual that every child embraced enthusiastically. She also ensured their highest

level of performance by scaffolding the activities that led them to the top.

The students were asked to

- discuss their field trip to the mayor's office (remember and understand);
- prepare (with Ms. Crista's modeling) a brainstorm and flow map about the events that they experienced, for instance, getting candy from the mayor's aide (understand and apply);

- decide which of the events they felt were most important to them (evaluate);
- write a paragraph explaining why they enjoyed their field trip (create).

GENERATIVE THINKING IN HIGH SCHOOL

Creative Writing

The poems in Table 6.1 demonstrate how that students can discover a little bit of their writer's voice through the inspiration of a short poem by Eloise Greenfield (1986) and the high expectations of their teachers. The following original poems were *created* by three ninth graders on their first day in one of my high school creative writing classes.

Table 6.1   Modeling Poetry for Student Writers

Love don't mean all that kissing
Like on television
Love means Daddy
Saying keep your mama company
    till I get back
And me doing it.
            —E. Greenfield (1986)

Love don't mean sitting
and holding hands like in a movie.
Love means
Seeing someone I care about
Hurting
And me trying to comfort him.
            —Cara

Fear don't mean
creatures under you bed.
Fear means the flinch of a giant
fist
    bearing down on you
when you were young.
            —Jake

Love don't mean spring bursting
Like on a Paris postcard.
Love means me becoming tipsy
from the smell of his familiar
    laundry detergent
And an occasional tickle.
            —Sarah Beth

American History

Ms. Mindy's *Three Presidents Research Project* stimulated students to higher thinking because Ms. Mindy developed a project that expected students to succeed. She invited students to

- work in groups of three;
- conduct research on Washington, Adams, and Jefferson;
- analyze important domestic and foreign policies as well as successes and failures of each president;

- evaluate the performance of each president and, using specific examples, decide who were the most successful and least successful at the time and why;
- decide who would be the best president for today, using two current issues to make their decision;
- create a slide show or trifold display to complement class presentation.

World Literature

After a unit on mythology, challenge students to create a *biofile* for a 21st century mythological creature, god, mortal, or similar character. Their project would include

- physical description and special features;
- current dwelling and origin;
- personal traits, qualities, habits, characteristics, weaknesses, strengths, likes, dislikes;
- what the character explains about nature or mankind.

Stretch their thinking further by asking them to describe the ways their characters help or harm a current societal problem, for example, poverty or global warming.

MS. MINDY'S STORY

I was delighted when one group of students presented its report as a theatrical production titled *Three Good Men*.

They decorated, designed, and cut out a trifold display to serve as a puppet stage on which appeared a paper witch (fastened to a popsicle stick) who introduced the lesson/performance: "Double, double, toil and trouble. Make three men pop out of a bubble."

Suddenly three paper puppet masks of Washington, Adams, and Jefferson (which were also fastened to popsicle sticks) appeared. "Backstage" voices of students argued over which of the three had been the best president. The paper witch once again appeared, this time demanding, "Double, double, toil and trouble. Make three men pop out of a big bubble."

Donning their presidential popsicle masks, the three students walked from behind the cardboard cutout stage to present their decision concerning which of the three first presidents would be the best president today.

Another group thought way outside the box by creating a presidential ticket of Jefferson and Obama. The issues they used were abortion and war; they cited effectively Jefferson's views on individual rights as well as his belief in neutrality, which he tried to continue through Washington's Neutrality Proclamation.

I believe the three presidents research project was successful because I offered students the strategies they needed to be successful and provided them a detailed assignment sheet that included a rubric so they would know how I was going to score them. I believe it is important to be very clear about expectations for an assignment, especially if it is a performance-based assignment. I also think it is helpful to encourage students to have fun, even high school students. Often I will say, "You all know I love to give extra credit for students who go above and beyond the parameters of the assignment." Even though my extra credit may only be a few points, many students go for it. Letting students know that assignments—and learning—can be fun makes the presentation of information and conclusions all the more interesting and memorable for the entire class.

Art and Advertising

Have students use software like Microsoft Office Publisher to create a postcard that attractively presents information learned in any subject area. For example, students learning about theorems in geometry might write on one side of the postcard a testimonial on behalf of Euclid, telling us on why he created geometry, how he devised the branch of mathematics, and how it has improved our lives. On the other side of the postcard, they can design a layout that includes one of the proofs covered in the unit.

Grab Bags to Generate Thinking at All Grade Levels

Political leaders can expound all they want to convince students (and teachers) that belief in high-stakes testing, timelines, and textbooks is just good, old-fashioned, common sense. Their shouting is useless. As Einstein knew instinctively, and brain research verifies: "Common sense is the collection of prejudices acquired by age eighteen." Emotions are key players in thinking processes (Zull, 2004) and especially so in adolescents. Until their prefrontal lobes mature, adolescents respond to the emotional prodding of their amygdalae, not their prefrontal cortical cortexes (Wolfe, 2001). Consequently, the use of the grab bag strategy is likely to inspire generative thinking more readily than questions at the end of textbook chapters. Why? Because the novel, gamelike quality of grab bags is more likely to spark student interest and willingness to work at demonstrating their understanding of specific objectives.

> Common sense is the collection of prejudices acquired by age eighteen.
>
> —Albert Einstein

The grab bag strategy is simple in concept but complex in the benefits it offers, calling to mind another of Einstein's insights: "Everything should be made as simple as possible, but not simpler." Consider the possibilities grab bags offer all teachers, not just language arts teachers. For example, science teachers can write atrium, ventricle, oxygenated blood, veins, and other terms into a bag. They can instruct groups of students to choose one part of the cardiovascular system for each student member in their group and transform the chosen parts as the cast of characters for the reality show, "Cardiovascular System in the House." The students-turned-actors will write lines for their shows, which will be evaluated by their audiences (i.e., other students), who will use specific criteria science teachers and their students have developed (see Chapter 5) to determine whether the shows clearly explain how the cardiovascular system works. In other words, student groups must gather information and mentally process it to generate creative products that represent their acquired learning about, in this case, the circulatory system.

Making Generative Thinking Happen

To make generative thinking happen, we must have a holistic, big-picture understanding of our curricular objectives. Expecting students to be generative thinkers does not find teachers directing students to answer questions at the end of textbook chapters. This dead-end activity does not appeal to any brain-centered principle particularly the novelty necessary to keep students emotionally engaged with learning. Answering questions at the end of chapters is no way to engage students of the twenty-first century, who routinely experience a bombardment of sensory input. If we hope to get our students succeeding on the barrage of high-stakes tests they must take, tests that allegedly assess proficiency, we need to ensure our students engage in generative thinking. By designing activities that foster critical thinking skills, we help them increase their neural connections and pathways to solve problems and master concepts instead of minutiae.

By using writing to teach math, social studies, science, and other subjects, we can expect our students to become generative thinkers.

Math. Present students with algebraic equations and then challenge them to become lawyers who must write their legal arguments to defend their answers to algebraic equations.

Social Studies. Before beginning a unit on ancient Asia, let students know they will be expected to design a cereal box whose front must display the khan or sultan they believe worthy of cereal-champion fame. Make learning engaging enough and students will work in *and* out of class. Students willingly read their textbooks to learn to gather information on Genghis Khan, Shah Jahan, and other leaders if they see a worthwhile payoff. Ultimately, the brain and how it likes to learn has everything to do with student achievement. For the sides of the boxes, students can include interesting facts about their chosen celebrities such as words and terms popular during their time period, famous battles, and accomplishments. The back can be reserved for a timeline depicting their reign as well as their greatest accomplishments, defeats, and impact on their countries and cultures.

Science. Teacher can increase student interest in current events assignments as well as work quality by inviting them to report science news they have researched as if they were school newspaper reporters.

STUDENT TIMES
Science News

Killer Snail Venom Made Into Medicine!

Cone Snails Are Deadly But Helpful!

Venom That's a Medicine?

READING, WRITING AND GENERATIVE THINKING

Stimulate student's thinking by inviting them to write about the stories, chapters, or books they read in ways that challenge their creativity and critical thinking skills. Countless summaries on any topic or book are available on the Internet. If we continue to require traditional reports, we risk reading reports that demonstrate copy and paste skills and little else. The following report options can be used by teachers of all grade levels and subjects. (Adjust word choice of the directions so they are appropriate for your students.)

Although the activities listed mention books as the reading source, you can easily replace books with stories, chapters, downloaded resources, textbook sections, and other materials, a point illustrated in the first activity.

Figure 6.2   Fact-Based Call-Out Balloons

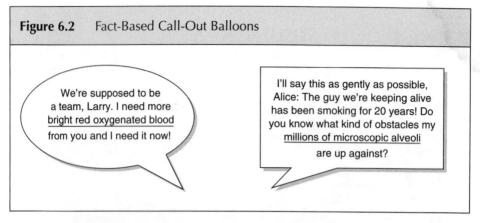

- Draw comic strip frames (minimum of eight) that summarize the book's plot or the essential information found in resources you downloaded from the Internet related to the cardiovascular system. If you want to keep the illustrations separate from text your characters (e.g., Atrium Alice or Larry Lung) are saying, identify the frames to which the text belongs and indicate with call-out balloons (see Figure 6.2). Each frame must include a minimum of two facts.
- Write a poem that communicates the book's theme (or meaning).
- Interview the main character in the book. Include both questions and answers.
- Write a letter to a friend recommending the book.
- Write a letter to the main character of the book, advising him or her on how to deal with other characters, how to cope with conflicts, and how to plan a course of action.
- Write a different story ending from the original. (This activity not only engages higher order thinking but also allows students to use writing to express and satisfy their emotions.)
- Explain why you would or wouldn't want to have one of the characters from the book as a friend.
- Write a newspaper article about the main events in the book as if it happened today. Include eyewitnesses or investigators (e.g., police, scientists) who conjecture why the events happened.

Headline News: Teacher Expecting
Generative Thinkers Gets Big Payoff!

I hope every teacher has experienced the satisfying payoff that comes from working hard to learn about our students and our standards. The payoff that comes from working as teacher-researchers who design units with activities that harness student engagement and promote higher level thinking for all. Such is the case for the unit *And Now the News*.

Today's brains respond and rely on media stimulation more than ever before. The communication tools they rely on provide them immediate information, communication, comfort, and stimulation. *And Now the News* capitalizes on student familiarity and interest by turning classrooms into media corporations. Grounded in standards-based objectives, the quarter-long, semester-long, or year-long unit casts students as news and investigative reporters, television news anchors, reality and talk-show hosts and casts. (For a year-long media environment, the corporation could include publishing houses, magazines, court TV shows, and so on—anything deemed useful to fulfilling objectives.)

Calling All Teachers!

Transforming your classroom into a media corporation establishes a novel learning environment that does more than stimulate student interest and higher-level thinking. The environment helps you satisfy another research-based feature of effective instruction, namely Feature 2: helping students make connections across curriculum and life. Viewed in a media way, you have become the CEO of a brain-centered framework for student achievement. (Remember to invite students to help name your corporation's newspaper, television network call letters, advertising agency, and so on.)

Setting Up the Corporation

The following list relates to language arts curricular objectives (e.g., literary response, writing a summary). However, media environments benefit the teachers from all subject areas who understand the value of integrating oral and written communication into their classrooms.

- Reading selections are chosen for their applicability to curricular objectives being satisfied.
- Students select the name of the corporation for which they work.
- Students role-play a variety of media "voices" (e.g., news reporters, anchors, talk show hosts).
- Students learn writing skills in multiple lesson types (see Chapter 3) as they experience the "real-life" situations and challenges relevant to their "jobs."

> Imaginative teachers have always used multiple approaches to the curriculum in order to open as many cognitive doors as possible.
>
> —Robert Sylwester

The CEO's Plan for Generative Thinking

Tables 6.2 and 6.3 contain activities from an instructional unit that used an abridged version of Stephen Crane's "The Open Boat" (Random House, 1986) and a teacher-prepared summary to move students up the ladder of higher level thinking as well as to satisfy a variety of seventh-grade language arts curricular objectives. Embedding novelty in vocabulary and grammar activities like the grab bag and case-solving activities comes in handy on substitute-teacher days. Novel activities help keep students connected to topics on which they have been working and help substitute teachers keep students on task.

Table 6.2	Generative Thinking Activities	
Category	**Bloom's Taxonomy**	**Product**
Vocabulary Writing a summary	Remembering Understanding Applying	*Teacher prepared summary.* To introduce the unit, the teacher prepares a summary of an abridged version of Crane's "The Open Boat" and incorporates into the summary words from the students' (required) vocabulary workbook to ensure the words are relevant to students.
		After discussing the words' meanings, the students write sentences of their own that use the words correctly.
	Analyze	After reading the story summary and before using dictionaries, students *deduce* the meaning of the words by using contextual clues from the story.
		After discussing the words' meanings, the students write sentences of their own that use the words correctly.
Vocabulary Writing a summary	Remembering Understanding Applying Creating	*Headline and news lead.* Students select and use vocabulary words in news reports they write (as well as in future news and television reporting assignments).

SUMMARY OF "THE OPEN BOAT"

Instructions

✎ Read the summary of Crane's story carefully. Think about each underlined word and its possible meaning in context to the story.

✎ Look up the dictionary definition to confirm the meaning of each word.

✎ Write a simple definition of each term in your notebook using your own words.

"The Open Boat" is a story a *catastrophe* at sea. A captain and his crew were able to *eject* themselves from the ship before it went down, surviving by the aid of their lifeboat.

The *onslaught* of waves from the storm must have been terrible, because as soon as one wave passed, another would come.

The survivors, fortunately, were never *disputatious*; they were, instead, always cooperative. The captain, therefore, didn't worry about his crew becoming *insubordinate*. They did everything he asked.

When they spotted land, their hopes *flourished*. They hoped to *outstrip* the storm and make it to shore safely. The *nub* of their problem, however, was the height of the breaking waves. The captain believed it was *prudent* to hold onto the capsized lifeboat, but the high seas *forced* them to jump into the ocean and attempt a *desperate* swim to shore.

Just as a courageous man swam towards the life boat, a huge wave *simultaneously* lifted the forlorn crew up and into shallow water, *quenching* everyone's thirst for safety.

Teacher Tip

Don't ask students to write definitions word-for-word from the dictionary. Such assignments don't represent authentic use of the dictionary, nor are they brain-compatible or writing-friendly.

NEWSCASTING

Instructions

✏ Read/discuss the abridged version of "The Open Boat" by Stephen Crane.*

✏ Identify the five W's (Who, What, When, Where, Why) in the story.

Working in small groups, create a news story based on "The Open Boat" that will be "broadcast" live. Roles will include a reporter—live on the scene—one or more eyewitnesses, one or more victims, a director, anchor, and script consultants. Incorporate a minimum of three events from "The Open Boat" into your news report.

After your group has prepared a draft script to submit to your "CEO" (your teacher), we'll have a conference to discuss ideas for refining your script. Once we're happy with the revisions, groups will begin rehearsing their "live" performance for the 10 O'Clock News.**

Vocabulary Connection

In groups, discuss what you believe to be the meaning of the underlined words in the following summary. Then look up the word in the dictionary to confirm its meaning.

*This exercise can be applied to any short story that lends itself to a news format.

**Follow up each "live" performance with a feedback session.

Category	Bloom's Taxonomy	Product
Vocabulary Sentence Fluency	Remembering Understanding Applying	Complex sentences. Students select and use vocabulary words and coordinating conjunctions (see News Reporter's Grab Bag) to write complex sentences that relate to the story. Who/whom practice (See the *Case of Who or Whom Solved!)*
Response to Literature		*Headline and news lead.* Students practice the skill of summary writing by writing a news story related to main events from the abridged version of Crane's "The Open Boat." Students include the following story elements: • A headline • A lead, answering who, what, where, when, and (the preliminary thoughts about) why the boating mishap occurred • A conclusion that conveys the boating mishap is under investigation

Table 6.3 Generative Thinking Activities

The Key to Success

Because students who are generative thinkers often talk about the *fun* they are having in your class, you may want to send a notice home or post it on your Web site, stating the curriculum objectives covered by your stimulating (and fun style of) teaching!

If we expect our students to be generative thinkers, we must know our students and how to teach them. We must systematically plan engaging lessons that are emotionally and intellectually stimulating. We must design activities that connect to our students' memories helping make learning a memorable experience.

Think media and writing *beyond* language arts classroom. Students will embrace the "jobs" you assign, and you will nurture generative thinking. Maybe you are a science teacher who will ask students to write a feature medical report concerning a man who had a heart attack. What happened in

NEWS REPORTER'S GRAB BAG

For students: Reporters use coordinating conjunctions to help them report news to their readers. Today you will practice using conjunctions to write sentences that will help you write more authentic news stories.

For teachers: Place words in two separate grab bags that you draw on your board, smart board, or student handouts.

Creating Complex Sentences— Vocabulary Grab Bag

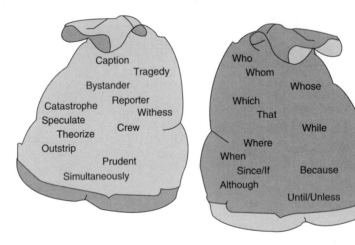

Left bag:
Caption
Tragedy
Bystander
Catastrophe Reporter
Speculate Withess
Theorize Crew
Outstrip
Prudent
Simultaneously

Right bag:
Who
Whom
Whose
Which
That
While
Where
When
Since/If Because
Although
Until/Unless

Instructions

➥ Choose one word from the left bag and one from the right.

➥ Write a sentence that correctly combines the two words, completing the sentence with additional words of your choice.

➥ Repeat the exercise five times using different words from the grab bags for each sentence. Check off words in the grab bags as you use them and underline them in your sentences.

➥ Combine the five sentences into a cohesive paragroph.

Teacher Tip

Vocabulary activities such as these are very useful for substitute-teacher days. They're easy to facilitate and can help kids stay on task with the planned curriculum despite your absence.

THE CASE OF WHO OR WHOM—SOLVED!

Remembering the cases of pronouns will help you know whether to use who or whom.

Pronouns

Nominative Case: who	I/we	he/she	they
Objective Case: whom	me/us	him/her	them

How to solve the case of who or whom
    Rework a clause or question into statements that use a pronoun from each case.

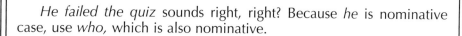

Example 1. The boy (who, whom) failed the quiz stayed for extra help.
    Statement 1.   <u>Him</u> failed the quiz.
    Statement 2.   <u>He</u> failed the quiz.

He failed the quiz sounds right, right? Because *he* is nominative case, use *who*, which is also nominative.

Example 2. The boy (who, whom) I argued with apologized.
    Statement 1. I argued with <u>he</u>.
    Statement 2. I argued with <u>him</u>.

I argued with him sounds better, and because *him* is objective case, use *whom,* which is also objective case.
    Helpful hint. Notice only objective case pronouns contain the letter "m." Maybe that will help you, too.

TRY IT OUT!

Underline the correct word, using sentences from your news leads.

1. The mechanic, (who, whom) was known as the oiler, eventually drowned.

2. The captain, (who, whom) they trusted completely, successfully determined the best time to head for shore.

3. The reporter (who, whom) the man saved was rushed to the hospital for observation.

4. The captain returned the blanket to the bystander to (who, whom) it belonged.

5. (Who, Whom) will you work with for your news presentation?

his circulatory system that caused the attack, and how could it have been prevented? Maybe you are a history teacher who asks students to interview a famous figure from the past.

The choices we have on how to generate higher levels of thinking in our students are limited only by our imaginations (and those of our students) and our willingness to plan outside the classrooms so that we provide students the tools to do the work inside the classroom. Talk with your students. Ask them how they want to learn and they will learn—because you make learning hard work but fun every day.

QUESTIONS FOR REFLECTION

1. What strategies do you use to hook learners?

2. In what ways do you ensure you are helping students use higher levels of thinking?

3. What issues, topics, and formats will encourage your students as generative thinkers? Have you asked their opinions lately?

4. Regarding the brain-compatible framework for student achievement, how does the feature of effective instruction related to generative thinking harmonize with

   ● Brain-Compatible Principles 3 and 4: novelty; memory?
   ● Core Propositions 1 and 4: commitment to students and their learning; systematic thinking about best practice and learning from experience?

7 Fostering Cognitive Collaboration

*When education is based upon experience, and educative
experience is seen to be a social process. . . . The teacher loses the
position of external boss or dictator but takes on
that of leader of group activities.*
—John Dewey, *Experience and Education*

Feature 6

Classrooms foster cognitive collaboration.

Chapter 7 explores how effective teachers foster cognitive collaboration
in their classrooms and advance student achievement by doing so.
Regarding the brain-compatible framework for student achievement, Feature
6 harmonizes with

- Brain-Compatible Principles 1–4: safety; respect; novelty; memory;
- Core Propositions 1 and 5: commitment to students and their learning and learning communities. (See Table 7.1.)

Figure 7.1   Cognitive Collaboration

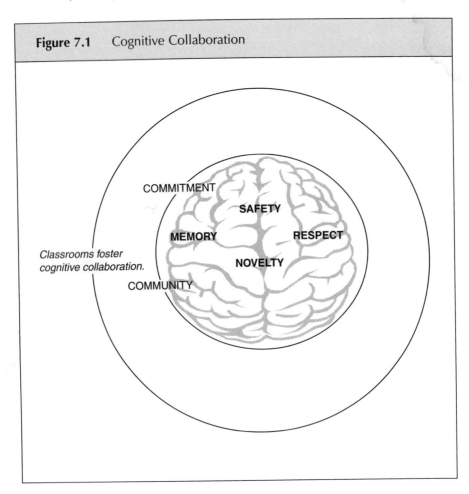

CHARACTERISTICS OF FEATURE 6

Research from the National Research Center on English Language & Achievement showed effective teachers nurtured students, most of them from poor and diverse populations, to beat the odds (Langer, 2000, 2004) and succeed on high-stakes tests. Among the patterns emerging from the research was the feature suggesting that effective teachers consistently created and sustained collaborative atmospheres within their classrooms.

Students regularly worked in small and large groups. Effective teachers routinely encouraged students to share their ideas and responses. Learning was a social activity, whereby students were permitted to question and challenge each other's ideas and, having done so, create new responses. Effective teachers provided support, moving from group to group, modeling questions and comments that fostered deeper discussions and analyses.

Language differences were not barriers. From the very beginning of the school year, effective teachers established seating plans that grouped English language learners with native speakers, setting high expectations of social interaction grounded by supportive atmospheres.

MARIA'S STORY

I will never forget the day I met Maria. The teacher whom I was observing met me at the door saying it was the worst day in the world for her to be observed because she had a new little girl who was terrified. It was the first day of school for the non-English-speaking Maria, who had arrived from Guadalajara the day before. (I learned this from my [Spanish] conversation with mom, who sat with Maria outside the classroom.) Maria begged her mama to stay and was breaking my heart with her tears and crying. The teacher asked the mom to enter the classroom and sit by Maria a few minutes. When the mother left, Maria sat at the table alone. The remaining children in the class were seated four to five at a table. There were empty seats at each table.

When the mother left, Maria sat quietly, stifling occasional whimpers. I got up from my chair and slipped into a chair near Maria, leaning to make smiling eye contact. When she asked me where the *baño* was, I walked her to the bathroom in the rear of room. Maria reached for my hand and held it as she returned to her seat.

Later Maria stared at the worksheet on penmanship the teacher put in front of her and then looked at me. I leaned over and told her (in my minimal Spanish) to write her name and the letter indicated on each line. She had an exceptionally beautiful, calligraphy-like handwriting. Maria periodically peered at other students to see what they were doing. When the teacher, who spoke no Spanish, announced recess, she asked three little girls to stay near Maria. They immediately rushed to Maria and two took her by the hand. As they lined up, I counted aloud: "Uno, dos, tres, cuatro amigas!" Then I repeated in English: "One, two, three, four friends!" All the girls beamed, including Maria. Ignoring my apology for getting involved, the teacher repeatedly thanked me for staying with Maria.

REFLECTING ON THE BRAIN-COMPATIBLE FRAMEWORK AND FEATURE 6

Maria's story initiates the reflection on Feature 6 in relation to the brain-compatible framework for high-stakes testing classrooms. Maria was a bright little girl who, understandably upset, had the real need to belong. As soon as she interacted with other children her age, she relaxed; she felt safer. When I visited the school the next day, I surreptitiously stopped by Maria's classroom. I saw her seated in a group with the three little girls from the previous day. She was smiling and speaking. The other girls were smiling and speaking as well. I am not sure of the language they spoke, but the scene suggested a collaborative bond, more social than intellectual, and it was working.

Maria demonstrates the brain's essential need for safety before learning can take place, a need satisfied, in part, through collaboration. Seating arrangement also plays a role in fostering the cognitive collaboration associated with student achievement.

Moving desks into groups, circles, pairs, or groups of three, four, or more to construct learning environments suggests effective teachers uphold Core Proposition 1. For example, what teachers would expend the energy moving desks or tables unless they were committed to students and their learning?

That effective teachers take time to ensure every group is contributing and valued, thereby demonstrating the brain-compatible principle of respect. Establishing collaborative groups that expect productive problem-solving social interaction demonstrates teachers care about their students as contributing members of our society as well. Engaging students in collaborate work intuitively (or purposefully) helps students develop the social skills necessary in the twenty-first century where high-functioning teamwork has become a workplace imperative for organizational success.

By supporting cognitive collaboration through small- and whole-group instructional settings, effective teachers demonstrate understanding of the learning brain's need for novelty. The conversations, the questions, the collaborative activities they design represent interesting and challenging activities that create positive emotional states that increase real learning opportunities.

Sylwester (1995) offered insight into why whole group and small group collaboration fosters student learning and achievement on high-stakes tests for students:

> The brightest students are the ones who always have their hands in the air to expand the discussion through stories about their own experience: They unconsciously maintain and extend their own memory networks through active recall. It's as if their brains know how important it is for them to act on their knowledge and beliefs, to not sit passively by and let their classmates make all of the mental connections. (p. 103)

Effective teachers demonstrate an intuitive or knowledge-based understanding of *distributed intelligence*, the concept that intelligence is not limited to one body, one mind. Rather our intelligence increases every time we access and use information from our environment, technology (Hoerr, 2006), and other people (Crawford, 2007). Thus, by establishing and sustaining classroom settings and developing plans that foster cognitive collaboration, effective teachers help students harness their existing memories and tap into and build upon them, influencing critical thinking skills that ensure their success.

THE BRAIN-COMPATIBLE FRAMEWORK WITH FEATURE 6 IN ACTION

The compatibility of brain-compatible principles with NBPTS propositions and Feature 6 suggests that collaborative learning works. Confirming what brain-compatible teachers know about effective instruction, the findings make it that much more difficult to support the federally sanctioned remediation programs that pull students who do not learn within established timelines out of socially and intellectually diverse classrooms and push them into remedial classes arranged in rows of isolation.

A Case Against Remedial Classrooms

Aimed at improving student achievement records, remediation classes are counterintuitive to authentic learning that occurs in naturally diverse classroom settings. Students needing extra help are much more likely to access that help from students in the classrooms from which they are pulled.

The Learning Pyramid (see Figure 7.2) illustrates that greatest learning retention occurs when students teach each other. The pyramid offers insight into why collaborative settings like the ones described in feature 6 may have a positive influence on student achievement. Stated simply, students retain longer what they learn by discussing, doing, and teaching. As Sousa (2006a) so aptly put it, "Whoever explains, learns" (p. 95).

A Case Against Gifted Classrooms

Another program difficult to support in light of what research suggests about collaboration and student achievement is the gifted program, the kind that removes students identified as gifted from regular classroom settings and provides them with separate, or *gifted*, instruction as if the novelty-hungry brains of all students wouldn't relish such opportunity! Separate

Figure 7.2 The Learning Pyramid

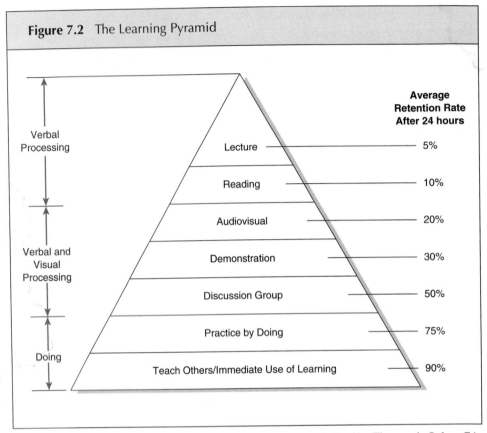

SOURCE: Sousa, D. A. (2006). *How the Brain Learns* (3rd ed.). Thousand Oaks, CA: Corwin Press.

instructional settings potentially do not help but harm our best and brightest students. Separated from natural, intellectually diverse classroom settings, gifted students do not learn important social and leadership skills necessary to successfully contribute to the future intellectually diverse workplaces in which they will compete.

Isolated from their intellectually different peers, gifted students are robbed of the learning opportunity inherent in teaching others already illustrated by the Learning Pyramid. Moreover, without the need to teach less advanced peers, gifted students are denied opportunities to develop important life skills, such as patience, tact, diplomacy, and compassion. The damage of the programs is exacerbated by teachers who refer to their gifted students as their "smart" kids, their "gifted" students fostering an elitist attitude that may serve them poorly. When they face real world challenges in college and beyond, will they be problem solvers comfortable with reaching out for support, or will they become frustrated and angry with the realization they aren't as gifted as they were led to believe?

NBPTS Core Proposition 5 and Collaboration

Core Proposition 5 relates to teachers recognizing the responsibility and benefits derived from collaboration with *their* learning community. Nonetheless, I have taken the liberty to discuss it here because by becoming active members of our learning communities, we may be able to help groups of students who are being removed from regular classes in the name of student achievement.

Armed with research-based information about the benefits collaborative settings have on student achievement, we have the knowledge base to effectively

- argue against school and district programs that form homogeneous groups of students, whether remedial or gifted;
- commit to promoting effective instruction that fosters student achievement for all;
- challenge instructional practices that make our students hate tests, hate school, hate learning.

If our vision of what learning should be, and could be, matches the higher performing classrooms that foster cognitive collaboration, then we may be ready to defend our vision to advocate on behalf of heterogeneous classrooms that provide students the collaborative instructional setting supported by research. That's exactly what NBPTS Core Proposition 5 is all about: teachers working with fellow educators to contribute to the effectiveness of school operations from instructional policy and programs to curriculum and staff development.

Making Feature 6 Happen

One of my fondest memories related to fostering learning communities within my classrooms comes from a year when I taught not only language arts but also social studies. I studied the content for which I was responsible and invited my student groups to answer the following: "If you were the teacher, how would you teach this unit? What kinds of activities, projects, homework, assessments, etc., would you plan?"

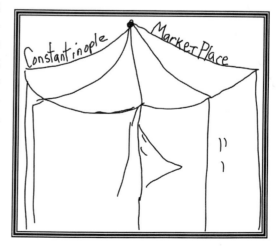

Each quarter a new class of students heard my questions and saw the chapter headings and topics related to my units on ancient Africa and Asian civilizations. During each quarter I used group ideas and interests to develop activities. Among my fondest memories was the class that was particularly amazed that salt was worth its weight in gold and seashells were used for barter. Lively and interesting class discussions led to their decision to transform our classroom into a Middle East marketplace.

Students moved desks around the perimeter of the room creating stands to trade candy, homemade soap, popcorn, old jewelry, baseball cards, and other goods. Money was forbidden. I gave each student five seashells with which to barter. Eventually they discovered some items had more trading power than others did, and one boy discovered he could barter his skills: ten push-ups for a cookie.

Imagine the insightful conversations and writing opportunities emerging from inviting students to compare ancient marketplaces to today's virtual marketplaces, such as Ebay. I imagine right along with you because Ebay was not a household word when I taught social studies. Still, what I value most from the memory is the learning success that occurred because I fostered a safe collaborative environment where I asked students to tell me how they wanted to learn, and I listened when they told me.

COLLABORATION AND SEATING ARRANGEMENTS

The collaborative approach promulgated by Feature 6 is reflected in many of the activities found in other chapters. For example, many of the activities in Chapter 6, which describes activities related to generative thinking, rely on cognitive collaboration. The "Getting to Know You" survey in Chapter 2 helps teachers establish productive learning groups and safe learning environments from the very beginning of the year. By sharing with students the *why* of moving them in and out of a variety of collaborative seating arrangements, we let our students know we are a team working together in our classroom learning communities. (If you think about how much time we teachers spend with our students, we really do have the potential to build learning communities on a daily basis.)

Arrangements conducive to peer conferencing look different from arrangements better suited to silent discussions or literature circles. Other configurations work best for story time or Socratic discussions. Keep in mind the intent of moving desks or tables is not to develop biceps but to foster the cognitive collaboration that promotes authentic learning experiences that foster student achievement.

Silence Is Golden

The silent discussion activity is particularly beneficial for students reluctant or resistant to speaking in small- and whole-group discussions as well as students with intrapersonal intelligence preferences. Silent discussions ensure all voices are "heard" and all students participate—safely.

- For each group you will need one large sheet of paper for each desk or table group and enough pens or pencils for each student.
- You will write a question in the center of the paper and cover the question with a sticky note (or something similar) until you are ready to begin the activity. The questions, relevant to your lesson or unit, may be different for each group or the same. (Encourage students not to peek.)
- Instruct students at each group area to stand during the activity, and remind them they may not speak during silent discussions.
- Tell students to remove sticky note and read their question. (Yes, some students will be reading upside down, so if they have difficulty, allow them to move so they can read more easily. The large sheets of paper on which the questions are written should be positioned upright in front of students who may have the most difficulty reading materials upside down or diagonally.)
- Tell students to write their responses to the question on the paper in a space on the paper directly in front of them.
- Provide students an appropriate amount of time, depending on the question and your observation of students' needs.
- Use a sound signal, such as a chime or bell, and direct students to rotate the paper. If you prefer, you can direct *students* to rotate clockwise (or counterclockwise) to a new position within the group. (Moving students instead of paper at elementary and middle school levels is the brain-friendly option that tends to the kinesthetic needs of younger learners.)
- Instruct students to read the response another member of the group has written and respond directly beneath the original response, agreeing, disagreeing, or expanding on the original idea.
- Repeat the process until all in the group have responded to at least two other student responses in the group.

High School. An English teacher who served on a districtwide committee on testing invited students to respond to a question about reading tests and *heard* important information from all students, information that was presented to the committee developing district benchmark tests.

- *The stories were too long!*
- *I agree. The whole test was too long and I got a headache.*
- *I think the reading benchmark was very dull because we had to read so much and only answer like 2 or 3 questions about that reading. It was very long, too long.*
- *I agree on the part that the stories were too long for the questions they asked. However, I think the questions shouldn't just try to ask the main point. They should make them sound meaningful.*

Middle School. A science teacher invited students to silently discuss global warming before they began a unit on weather and used the students' responses to generate K-W-L (i.e., what I know, want to know, learned) charts:

- *I think global warming is fake. Sure the world is getting hotter but earth has heated and cooled lots of time. If an ice cube melts in a glass of water, the water level does not go up.*
- *I think that it is not a good model because if you put a bunch of ice cubes in a glass of water the level rises. I don't agree.*
- *I don't know but I think that global warming stinks. We need to figure out some way to stop it. We also should figure out a way to prevent it in the future.*

No matter how you use silent discussions, you will recognize the value of the activity for the opportunity it affords all learners to contribute to discussions in ways usually reserved for a handful of students who routinely share ideas and opinions comfortably.

● ●

Physical changes such as seating changes that coincide with a change in subject or topic have been shown to enhance memory, making a marked impression on the brain, which can provide a sense of renewal as well as closure. This is why I have routinely rearranged seating at the beginning of each quarter, coinciding with changes in writing focus (e.g., description, narration, exposition, persuasion). Because our body/mind/memory connection is better engaged when information is absorbed through multiple modalities (e.g., spatial, kinesthetic, visual), I rely on peer interaction, movement, and seat and schedule changes to keep my classroom environment fresh and novel.

The charts on the following pages that depict various collaborative seating arrangements serve as examples of classroom floor plans that can help teachers who wish to foster cognitive collaboration in their classrooms. Remember, again, nothing suggested in this book is prescriptive. Implement only what makes sense to you as you strive to help your students achieve, as well as enjoy coming to your class every day.

Getting to Know You Groups

Grouping, or "chunking," learners together, five or six to a group, makes remembering student names easier and helps you establish learning-compatible teams. When we encourage dialogue between and among learners, *personal meaning* is enhanced, increasing the potential that material will be remembered.

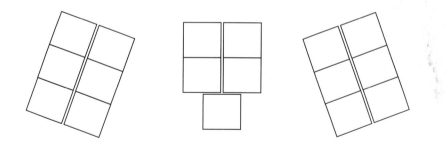

Pair-Share Seating

Grouping learners into pairs encourages peer feedback, an important element in facilitating writing improvement. As students demonstrate dependability, you may want to encourage them to move from designated seats to form additional partnerships that will enable them to give or get more feedback.

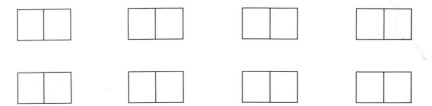

Good-Noise Groups

Once students know each other and you know them, large face-to-face grouping facilitates activities where students have full control over their learning. "Good" (versus loud and unproductive) noise levels peak at this time but so does authentic learning. When we allow learners to listen, talk, write, move around, analyze, problem solve, evaluate, and synthesize with others, they naturally tap into multiple learning styles and intelligences. Use *good-noise groups* for generative thinking activities that involve advertising agencies, ensembles of students presenting news reports, and other group-ings (see Chapter 6).

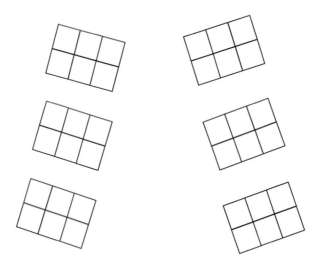

Face-Off Seating

Chunking students together on two different sides of the classroom physically encourages interpersonal communication and higher-level think-ing skills conducive to student participation in Socratic discussion, strategic planning, arguing causes, debating, thinking critically, and practicing real-life oral persuasion skills.

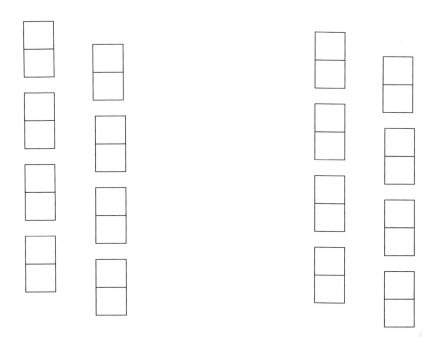

COGNITIVE COLLABORATION BEYOND THE CLASSROOM: COMMUNITY WRITING PARTNERS

The original project, called *Parents as Writing Partners*, began in 1988. Back then most of my students lived with both their parents. Over the years as society changed, I realized more and more of my students were using grand-parents, uncles, friends from after-school programs, and other people to serve as their home-writing partners. Of course, I always said yes to their choice of partners, but my students helped me realized the name of the project was inaccurate and that I needed to change the name to better reflect and honor those generous individuals who served as my students' writing partners (and who have my unending gratitude for their commitment to student learning).

Community Writing Partners is a weeklong project that can become one of your most rewarding experiences as a classroom teacher. Each student selects a partner from outside the classroom, for example, a willing parent, guardian, or neighbor, to serve as a community writing partner. The main objective is to help students reinforce the writing skills they have learned in class. Having experienced the opportunity to teach the writing process to others (see the Learning Pyramid) helps students improve their own writing skills. In the process something important happens. Students build a special bond with their community partner through the power of words. For students who participate, Community Writing Partners fosters collaboration and long-lasting memories that connect school with real life (see Chapter 2).

Let the Writing Begin!

Once students have experienced their own writing process several times in the classroom, I give them the invitation that announces the writing project.

● ●

COMMUNITY WRITING PARTNERS PROJECT

Greetings!

Please join me and my students in an exciting writing project!

You are invited to join our Writer's Workshop for days of experimentation and discovery. You will be guided by one of my students through the process of

- *choosing your own topic on which to write a short piece;*
- *brainstorming ideas and feelings about your topic;*
- *writing a draft;*
- *revising, editing, and producing a finished piece of prose or poetry.*

Because teaching is one of the best tools to learning, I am sure you can appreciate the value this project will have on my students as writers and effective communicators.

While in no way mandatory, I hope you will accept this opportunity to write a piece for our workshop and maybe even join us on Author's Day when you will be able to celebrate yourself as an author!

Thank you for considering the project, and I look forward to your response.

Sincerely,

● ●

Prepare Students to Become Partners

Before I let learners loose on their community partners, I remind them to use the same patience and encouragement they offer their peers during conferencing sessions. I give them a set of guidelines that we read and discuss together.

● ●

STUDENT GUIDELINES FOR COMMUNITY PARTNERS

HOW TO HELP YOUR PARTNER

- Help partner choose a topic to write about.

  ✐ a person   ✐ an event   ✐ a feeling

- Help partner brainstorm ideas and memories—filled with strong images.

- Help partner write a draft—prose or poetry. Write from dictation if your partner is too busy.

  ✐ Define and explain *line break* and *stanza* if poetry is chosen.

- Help partner conference, revise, and edit using workshop strategies.

- Help partner write a *final copy*. Again, write or type from dictation if your partner is too busy.

- Invite your partner to attend our *Authors' Day*.

● ●

Sometimes students adamantly contend that everyone they know is too busy to get involved. Over the years I have realized students often resist to mask their fear of disappointment should those they ask say no. The next day, however, most of these same protesters come back excitedly telling me they found a partner be it their mom, brother, uncle, or friend. I talk privately with any students who have not found outside partners, offering them a choice of me or various school community members who have agreed to lend support, other teachers, counselors, assistant principals. At that point, either of two things occurs: they choose the option I offer, or they make a stronger attempt to find someone.

This step in the process is an important one. During the first years of my project, I allowed students to do without a community partner. But when the day to share our writing came around (to be discussed shortly), students without partners appeared disappointed as they listened to peers read aloud their piece of writing *and* their partner's pieces, more so when the partners actually came to the day of sharing.

Celebrate the Results

Community members write stories that are often poignant. Over the years I have never tired of my "additional students." And I cannot help but ask myself: Would these adults, long out of school, have written their stories or poems without this project?

I recall a particular moment when one of my students began to cry while reading the poem he and his uncle had written. The boy asked, "Give me a moment please." The respectful silence my young seventh-grade students maintained while he composed himself remains to this day one of the proudest moments I have had as a teacher.

Authors' Day

The celebration of learning occurring on Authors' Day stands in sharp contrast to the ordeal of high-stakes testing occurring in today's classrooms.

The perfect setting in which to present the special pieces of writing is Authors' Day, the day at the end of each quarter set aside for sharing the works of students and their partners. I have always announced to my classes that I supply lollipops. Through the years various students and sometimes PTO funds have provided various treats ranging from cookies or chips to

---

LOURDES'S STORY

"The Headache Has Disappeared"

As I came out of my classroom still in a daze from my brain working as fast as the speed of light I wondered if I could ever learn the language I had set a goal to learn. Disheartened, I was asking myself if it was because I was too old or that I came from another culture that caused me not to learn anything that night.

This nightmare began five years ago when I took the determination to learn English. At first, the idea seemed simple, but it turned out to give me a headache. My first year of learning the language could be described by the words of confusion, frustration, and the strong desire of giving up. These emotions came from not understanding the teacher and not being able to express myself in English.

Even though learning a new language is a long life process, my writing and my reading skills are improving. As the time passed by, the patience, effort, and dedication paid off with the satisfaction of knowing that I can enjoy my English classes, conferences, and job training, realizing that the headache has disappeared.

EXCERPT FROM JIM'S STORY
"Fire"

Fire!!! You can almost feel the heat. Fire!!! Do you ever give it a second thought? I never did until October of 1957. . . .

I stood on that corner for what seemed like an eternity. Not reacting, not crying, just watching this macabre dance of flame destroy everything we owned. . . . We stood hugging and crying, the horrible feeling of having lost our home and the joyful feeling of being alive mixing together with our tears.

EXCERPT FROM LISA'S POEM
"Matters of Life and Death"

. . . A warm summer's day
the smell of a rose,
playing cards at the kitchen table
There is no good-bye
You live on in my heart.

veggies and dip. (From experience I recommend you stand by a Water Only rule because soda is unhealthy and juices stain.)

Your commitment to making the Community Writing Partners project take place in your classroom learning community will pay off when you witness its outcome. You will remember why you became a teacher and what brain-centered learning is all about.

QUESTIONS FOR REFLECTION

1. How do you foster cognitive collaboration in your classroom?

2. What sort of activities have you gotten involved in at your school or district?

3. How does Community Writing Partners reflect cognitive collaboration?

4. Regarding the brain-compatible framework for student achievement, how does the feature related to fostering cognitive collaboration harmonize with

   - Brain-Compatible Principles 1–4: safety; respect; novelty; memory?
   - Core Propositions 1 and 5: commitment to students and their learning and learning communities?

8 Envisioning Every Child as a Lifelong Learner

Teachers should know when their students are doing
(and learning) worthwhile things and when their students
are doing (and learning) things that will be damaging
to their personal and social development.

—Frank Smith
"Let's Declare Education a
Disaster and Get On With Our Lives"

The preceding parts of this book discussed the state of public education today, forever changed because of NCLB legislation that has defined student achievement through the lens of high-stakes testing results. Chapter 1 introduced the brain-compatible framework of student achievement to show readers how research on student achievement on high-stakes tests could be used to defend their brain-compatible best practice from the test practice that insinuates itself into their classrooms. Also introduced in Chapter 1 was a journey into the brain intended to help teachers and students discover together how the brain learns.

The six core chapters of this book discussed the researched-based features of effective instruction in terms of their harmony with brain-compatible practices. Each chapter described the characteristics of each feature and provided practical classroom examples and reflective questions. Descriptions, examples, and questions will not help today's high-stakes testing teachers unless we make some important decisions about the kind of teachers we hope to be.

In 1995 education scholar Frank Smith advised us to declare public education a disaster, a *Titanic*, doomed to sink under the weight of decades of solutions devised by well-intended meddlers. Smith suggested we abandon ship, seek refuge in child-centered lifeboats, and get on with our lives. More than a decade later, lifeboat students and teachers (those hoping to become or to maintain brain-compatible practices) endure whirling surges of legislated flotsam that threaten to sink our boats. Nonetheless, we row against the tide of test debris. We do not necessarily row because we believe in the legislated timeline that envisions all the nation's public school students proficient in reading and mathematics by 2014, qualifying each a place in Garrison Keillor's Lake Wobegone, where every child is above average. We row because we care about students; we care about teaching; we care about learning.

In spite of the temptation to give up, we teachers hold tight our oars and battle against the onslaught of testing wave after wave after wave because we know we steer our nation's children toward the safety of authentic brain-compatible learning and away from NCLB's high-stakes testing disaster.

The brain-compatible framework for student achievement is especially important because it is based on research on student achievement. This research can be used to resist the insistence of those who would have us implement teaching practices that conflict with what we, as brain-compatible teachers, know to be more authentic teaching practices.

Brain-compatible, child-centered teachers may be our nation's only hope against the sludge of political solutions that continually assault lifeboats of learning. By staying the course of brain-compatible teachers, we will succeed against the relentless assault of testing debris. Our full-fledged, brain-based assault against standardizing students will help us remain afloat in spite of the high-stakes testing debris we endure. Remember, the effective teachers who beat the odds helped their students succeed on tests by creating and sustaining authentic learning environments.

I hope this book has helped you think about student achievement beyond test scores and about becoming an effective teacher, a brain-compatible teacher who knows students need to feel safe, respected, engaged, and connected to their learning experiences so that the learning process becomes a wonderful story worth remembering.

I hope my brain-compatible framework for student achievement keeps you determined. We must not give up lest our students drown, clinging to thoughts of what learning might have been. Over a decade later, Frank Smith's image of lifeboat classrooms seems a prophecy. Let's imagine each of our classrooms a "sanctuary of teachers and students mutually engaged in sensible and productive activities, which are the sole justification for education" (p. 590).

STAY AFLOAT AND WRITE ON!

References and Further Readings

Abrams, L. M., & Madaus, G. F. (2003, November). The lessons of high-stakes testing. *Educational Leadership, 61*(3), 31–35.

Abrams, L., Pedulla, J., & Madaus, G. (2003, Winter). Views from the classroom: Teachers' opinions of statewide testing programs (1). *Theory into Practice 42*(1), 18–29.

Ackerman, R., & Mackenzie, S. (2006, May). Uncovering teacher leadership. *Educational Leadership, 63*(8), 66–80.

Adler-Baeder, F., Kerpelman, J. L., Schramm, D., Higginbotham, B., & Paulk, A. (2007, July). The impact of relationship education on Adolescents of Diverse Backgrounds. *Family Relations, 56*(3), 291–303.

Amrein, A. L., & Berliner, D. C. (2002, March 28). *High-stakes testing, uncertainty, and student learning.* Retrieved on May 22, 2003, from Educational Policy Analysis Archives.

Andersen, C. (2006). Drama. In S. Feinstein (Ed.), *The Praeger Handbook of Learning and the Brain* (Vol. 1, pp. 182–186). Westport, CT: Praeger.

Arizona Department of Education. (2005, November 1). *Standards-based teaching and learning: Academic K–12 standards.* Retrieved December 1, 2005, from http://www.ade.state.az.us

Armstrong, W. H. (1969). *Sounder.* New York: Harper Collins.

Atwell, N. (1990) *In the middle: Writing, reading, and learning with adolescents.* Portsmouth, NH: Heinemann.

Bailey, B. A. (2006). Classroom management. In S. Feinstein (Ed.), *The Praeger Handbook of Learning and the Brain* (Vol. 1, pp. 135–143). Westport, Conn: Praeger.

Bandura, A. (1986). Self-efficacy beliefs in human functioning. In *Social Foundations of Thought and Action.* Retrieved April 12, 2004, from http://www.emory.edu/EDUCATION/mfp/effpassages.html

Bandura, A. (1994). Self-efficacy. In V. S. Ramachaudran (Ed.), *Encyclopedia of human behavior* (Vol. 4, pp. 71–81). New York: Academic Press. (Reprinted in H. Friedman (Ed.), *Encyclopedia of mental health*. San Diego: Academic Press, 1998). Retrieved April 12, 2004, from Stanford University online Web site: http://www.emory.edu/EDUCATION/mfp/effpage.html

Barton, P. E. (2006, February). The dropout problem: Losing ground. *Educational Leadership, 63*(5), 14–18.

Berliner, D., & Biddle, B. (1995). *The manufactured crisis*. Reading, MA: Addison-Wesley.

Berliner, D., & Nichols, S. (2007). Collateral damage: How high-stakes testing corrupts America's schools. Cambridge: Harvard Education Press.

Berube, C. (2004, July/August). Are standards preventing good teaching? *Clearing House, 77*(6), 264–267.

Blodget, A. (2007, Spring). Beginning to learn. *Independent School, 66*(3), 62-74.

Bloomfield, D., & Cooper, B. (2003, May). NCLB: A new role for the federal government. *Technological Horizons in Education, 30*(10), S6–S9.

Boaler, J. (2003, March). When learning no longer matters: Standardized testing and the creation of inequality. *Phi Delta Kappan, 84*(7), 502–506.

Bracey, G. W., & Molnar, A. (2003, February). *Recruiting, preparing and retaining high quality teachers: An empirical synthesis*. Retrieved May 11, 2006, from Arizona State University, Education Policy Studies Laboratory at College of Education Web site.

Brady, R. (2003, January). *Can failing schools be fixed?* Retrieved October 6, 2004, from Thomas B. Fordham Foundation Web site.

Brain Connection (n.d.). http://www.brainconnection.com/

Brendtro, L. K., & Longhurst, J. E. (2006). At-risk behavior. In S. Feinstein (Ed.), *The Praeger Handbook of Learning and the Brain* (Vol. 1, pp. 81–91). Westport, Conn: Praeger.

Brown, C. (2002, March). *Opportunities and accountability to leave no child behind in the middle grades: An examination of the No Child Left Behind Act of 2001*. Retrieved November 14, 2004, from the Edna McConnell Clark Foundation Web site.

Carpenter, J. (Writer/Director).(1978). *The Fog* [Motion picture]. Unted States Avco Embassy & E.D.I.

Caskey, M., & Ruben, B. (2003, December). Research for awakening adolescent learning. *Education Digest 69*(4), 36–38.

Cavalluzzo, L. C. (2004, November). *Is National Board Certification an effective signal of teacher quality?* The CAN Corporation.

Cherniss, C. (1997). Teacher empowerment, consultation, and the creation of new programs in schools. *Journal of Educational & Psychological Consultation, 8*(2), 135–152.

Clarke, M., Shore, A., Rhoades, A., Abrams, L., Miao, J., & Li, J. (2003, January). *Perceived effects of state-mandated testing programs on teaching and learning: Findings from interviews with educators in low-, medium-, and high-stakes states* (Boston College, Lynch School of Education). Retrieved November 11, 2004, from the National Board on Educational Testing and Public Policy Web site.

Clementson, J. J. (2006). Information processing model. In S. Feinstein (Ed.), *The Praeger Handbook of Learning and the Brain* (Vol. 1, pp. 256–262). Westport, Conn: Praeger.

Cozolino, L. & Sprokay, S. (2006, Summer). Neuroscience and adult learning. *New Directions for Adult & Continuing Education.* 110, 11–19.

Crane, S. The open boat in *Random House achievement program in literature.* (1986). New York: Random House.

Crawford, G. B. (2007). *Brain-based teaching with adolescent learning in mind* (2nd ed.). Thousand Oaks, CA: Corwin Press.

Creswell, J. W. (2002). *Educational research: Planning, conducting, and evaluating quantitative and qualitative research.* Upper Saddle River, NJ: Pearson.

Darling-Hammond, L. (2003, May). Keeping good teachers: Why it matters, what leaders can do. *Educational Leadership, 58*(8), 7.

Dewey, J. (1938/1997). *Experience and education.* New York: Touchstone Books.

Diamond, M., & Hopson, J. (1998). *Magic trees of the mind: How to nurture your child's intelligence, creativity, and healthy emotions from birth through adolescence.* New York: Dutton.

Draganski, B., Gaser, C.; Busch, V., Schuierer, G., Bogdahn, U., & May, A. (2004, January 22). Neuroplasticity: Changes in grey matter induced by training. *Nature, 427*(6972), 311–312.

Education Trust. (2004, October). *Measured progress: States are moving in the right direction in narrowing achievement gaps and raising achievement for all students, but not fast enough.* Retrieved October 17, 2004, from Education Trust Web site.

Eisner, E. (2005, September). Back to the whole. *Educational Leadership, 63*(1), 14–18.

Elementary and Secondary Education Act of 1965, 20 § 236–244 (1965).

Elmore, R. F. (2003, November). A plea for strong practice. *Educational Leadership, 61*(3), 6–10.

Evers, W., Brouwers, A., & Tomic, W. (2002, June). *Burnout and self-*

efficacy: A study on teachers' beliefs when implementing an innovative educational system in the Netherlands. Retrieved September 25, 2003, from EBSCOhost database.

Faulkner, W. (n.d.). Quotes and Poem.com. Retrieved March 10, 2007, from http://www.quotesandpoem.com/quotes/showquotes/author/william_faulkner/24417

Finneran, K. (Ed.). (2002–2003, Winter). Testy about testing [Editorial]. *Issues in Science and Technology, 19*(2), 41–42. Retrieved April 9, 2003, from ProQuest database.

Friedman, I. (2000, May). Burnout in teachers: Shattered dreams of impeccable professional performance. *Journal of Clinical Psychology, 56*(5), 595–606. Retrieved July 2, 2004, from EBSCOhost database.

Fuchs, L. S., & Fuchs, D. (1986, Spring). Curriculum-based assessment of progress toward long-term and short-term goals [Electronic version]. *Journal of Special Education, 20*(1), 69–82.

Gardner, H. (1985). *Frames of mind: The theory of multiple intelligences.* New York: Basic Books.

Gleason, B. (2004, November 22). ASCD adopts positions on high-stakes testing and the achievement gap. *ASCD Conference News.* Retrieved November 25, 2004, from Association for Supervision of Curriculum Development Web site.

Goldhaber, D. (2004, March). *Can teacher quality be effectively assessed?* Seattle: The University of Washington & the Urban Institute.

Goldstein, J., & Noguera, P. (2006, March). A thoughtful approach to teacher evaluation. *Educational Leadership, 63*(6), 31–36.

Greenfield, E. (1986). Honey, I love and other love poems. New York: Harper Trophy.

Gruenert, S. (2000). Shaping a new school culture. *Contemporary Education, 71*(2), 14-17.

Gunzenhauser, M. (2003, Winter). High-stakes testing and the default philosophy of education. *Theory into Practice, 42*(1), 51–58.

Hanson, A. (2005). No Child Left Behind: High-stakes testing and teacher burnout in urban elementary schools (Doctoral dissertation, University of Phoenix). Available at *Education Resource Information Center* (ERIC Document Reproduction Service No. ED493443).

Hanson, A. (2006). Writing. In S. Feinstein (Ed.), *The Praeger Handbook of Learning and the Brain* (Vol. 2, pp. 503–509). Westport, Conn: Praeger.

Hart. L. (1991, November). *Teaching to the Brain.* Association for Supervision and Curriculum Development *UPDATE,* Vol. 33 (8).

Harvey, J. (2003, November). The matrix reloaded. *Educational Leadership, 61*(3), 19–21.

Hess, F. (2003, November). The case of being mean. *Educational Leadership, 61*(3), 22–26.

Hodgkinson, H. (2002, December). Grasping demographics: Get ready for them now. *Education Digest, 68*(4), 4–7.

Hodgkinson, H. (2003, April). *Leaving too many children behind: A demographer's view on the neglect of America's youngest children.* Retrieved February 2, 2007, from Institute for Educational Leadership Web site: http://www.iel.org/pubs/oielp.html

Hoerr, T. (2006) Distributed intelligence. In S. Feinstein (Ed.), *The Praeger Handbook of Learning and the Brain* (Vol. 1, pp. 179–182). Westport, Conn: Praeger.

Immordino-Yang, M. H. (2005). A tale of two cases: Emotion and affective prosody after hemispherectomy. (Doctoral dissertation, Harvard University, 2005). Retrieved October 12, 2007, from *ProQuest Dissertations and Theses* database.

Jean Piaget Society (Web site). (2008). http://www.piaget.org/

Jensen, E. (2007). *Introduction to brain-compatible learning* (2nd ed.). Thousand Oaks, CA: Corwin Press.

Kellogg, J. S., Hopko, D. R., & Ashcraft, M. H. (1999). *Journal of Anxiety Disorders, 13*(6), 591–600.

Klein, K., & Boals, A. (2001, September). Expressive writing can increase working memory capacity. *Journal of Experimental Psychology, 130*(3), 520–533.

Kohn, A. (2005, September). Unconditional teaching. *Educational Leadership, 63*(1), 20–24.

Krashen, S. (2002). *Effective second language acquisition.* Torrance, CA: Staff Development Resources.

Krashen, S. (2003). *Explorations in language acquisition and use.* Portsmouth, NH: Heinemann.

Ku, I., & Plotnick, R. (2003, February). Do children from welfare families obtain less education? *Demography, 40*(1), 151–170.

Langer, J. A. (2000). Six features of effective instruction. Beating the odds: teaching middle school students to read and write well [Online report]. National Research Center on English Language & Achievement. Retrieved September 14, 2007, from http://www.albany.edu/cela/reports.html#L

Langer, J. A. (2004). *Getting to Excellent: How to create better schools.* New York: Teachers College Press.

Linden, D., Keijsers, G., Eling, P., & Schaijk, R. (2005, January). Work stress and attentional difficulties: An initial study on burnout and cognitive failures. *Work & Stress, 19*(1), 23–36.

Lubell, K. M., Kegler, S. R., Crosby, A. E., & Karch, D. (2007, September 7). Suicide trends among youths and young adults aged 10–24 years–United States, 1990–2004. *Morbidity and Mortality Weekly Report, Centers for Disease Control and Prevention, 56*(35), 905–908.

Luekens, M. T., Lyter, D. M., & Fox, E. E. (2004). *Teacher attrition and mobility: Results from the teacher follow-up survey, 2000–01* (NCES 2004–301). U.S. Department of Education, National Center for Education Statistics. Washington, DC: U.S. Government Printing Office.

Mandel, S. (2006, March). What new teachers really need. *Educational Leadership, 63*(6), 66–69.

Maslach, C. (1976). Burned out [Electronic version]. *Human Behavior, 5,* 16–22.

Maslach, C., Schaufeli, W. B., & Leiter, M. P. (2001). Job burnout. *Annual Review of Psychology, 52*(1), 397–422.

Mathison, S., & Freeman, M. (2003, September 24). Constraining elementary teachers' work: Dilemmas and paradoxes created by state mandated testing. *Education Policy Analysis Archives, 11*(34). Retrieved September 19, 2005, from http://epaa.asu.edu/epaa/v11n34/

Moon, T. R., Callahan, C. M., & Tomlinson, C. A. (2003, April 28). Effects of state testing programs on elementary schools with high concentrations of student poverty—good news or bad news? *Current Issues in Education,* [On-line] *6*(8).

Nathan, N. (2002, April). The human face of the high-stakes testing *story. Phi Delta Kappan, 83*(8), 595.

National Board for Professional Teaching Standards (Web site). (2007). http://nbpts.org

National Education Association. (2005). *Attracting and keeping quality teachers.* Retrieved October 30, 2005, from National Education Association Web site.

National Education Association. (2006). Stand up for children: Pontiac v. Spellings. Retrieved May 13, 2006, from National Education Association Web site: http://www.nea.org/lawsuit/index.html

Nitko, A. J. (2004). *Educational assessment of students* (4th ed.). Upper Saddle River: Pearson.

No Child Left Behind Act of 2001, Pub. L. 107–110, 20 U.S.C. § 6301 *et seq.* (2002) (enacted). Retrieved October 14, 2004, from http://www.ed.gov/policy/elsec/leg/esea02/107-110.pdf

Noddings, N. (2005, September). What does it mean to educate the whole child. *Educational Leadership, 63*(1), 8–13.

Orlich, D. C. (2004, September/October). No child left behind. An Illogical accountability model. *Clearing House, 78*(1), 6–11.

O'Sullivan, R. (2005, June). *Investigating the classroom assessment literacy of board certified teachers.* Chapel Hill, NC: University of North Carolina at Chapel Hill, the Western Region Education Service Alliance (WRESA), and the Assessment Training Institute (ATI).

Owens, R. G. (2004). *Organizational behavior in education: Adaptive leadership and school reform* (8th ed.). New York: Allyn & Bacon.

Pahnos, M. L. (1990, Fall). The principal as the primary mediator of school stress. *Education, 111*(1), 125–129.

Pedulla, J., Abrams, L., Madaus, G., Russell, M., Ramos, M., & Miao, J. (2003, March). *Perceived effects of state-mandated testing programs on teaching and learning: Findings from a national survey of teachers.* Boston College, Lynch School of Education. Retrieved November 11, 2004, from The National Board on Educational Testing and Public Policy Web site: http://www.bc.edu/research/nbetpp/reports.html

Perreault, G. (2000, Summer). The classroom impact of high-stress testing. *Education, 120*(4), 705–710.

Patterson, J. H., Collins, L., & Abbott, G. (2004, March). A study of teacher resilience in urban schools. *Journal of Instructional Psychology, 31*(1), 3–11.

Poe, E. A. (1975). The fall of the house of Usher. In *Stories from the four corners* (pp. 48–59). New York: Amsco Publishers.

Pogrow, S. (2006, November) Restructuring high-poverty elementary schools for success: A description of the hi-perform school design. *Phi Delta Kappan, 88*(3), 223–229.

Popham, J. (2004, September). Why assessment illiteracy is professional suicide. *Educational Leadership, 62*(1), 82–83.

Ravitch, D. (2003). *The language police: How pressure groups restrict what students know.* New York: Knopf.

Ravitch, D. (2006, January 5). 50 standards for 50 states is a formula for incoherence and obfuscation [Commentary]. Quality counts at 10: A decade of standards-based education. *Education Week, 25*(17), 54–58.

Reivich, K., & Shatte, A. (2002). *The resilience factor.* New York: Broadway Books.

Ronis, D. (2006). Assessment. In S. Feinstein (Ed.), *The Praeger Handbook of Learning and the Brain* (Vol. 1, pp. 74–81). Westport, Conn: Praeger.

Ross, C. A. (2006, Summer). Brain self-repair in psychotherapy: Implications for education. *New Directions for Adult and Continuing Education, 110*, 29–33.

Rothstein, R. (2004, November). The achievement gap: A broader picture. *Educational Leadership, 62*(3), 40–43.

Sapolsky, R. M. (2007). *Why zebras don't get ulcers* (3rd ed.). New York: Henry Holt and Company.

Short, P. M., & Greer, J. T. (2002). *Leadership in empowered schools: Themes from innovative efforts* (2nd ed.). Upper Saddle River, NJ: Merrill/Prentice-Hall.

Smethem, L., & Adey, K. (2005, August). Some effects of statutory induction on the professional development of newly qualified teachers: a comparative study of pre- and post-induction experiences. *Journal of Education for Teaching, 31*(3), 187–200.

Smilkstein, R. (2006). Constructivism. In S. Feinstein (Ed.), *The Praeger Handbook of Learning and the Brain* (Vol. 1, pp. 154–158). Westport, Conn: Praeger.

Smith, F. (1986). *Insult to intelligence*. Portsmouth, NH: Heinemann Educational Books.

Smith, F. (1991). *To think*. New York: Teachers College Press.

Smith, F. (1995, April). Let's declare education a disaster and get on with our lives. *Phi Delta Kappan, 76*(8), 584–590.

Smith, T. (2005, June). *An examination of the relationship between depth of student learning and National Board Certification status*. Boone, NC: Appalachian State University.

Sousa, D. (2006a). Forgetting. In S. Feinstein (Ed.), *The Praeger Handbook of Learning and the Brain* (Vol. 1, pp. 228–231). Westport, Conn: Praeger.

Sousa, D. A. (2006b). *How the brain learns* (3rd ed.). Thousand Oaks, CA: Corwin Press.

Sprenger, M. (2007). *Becoming a "Wiz" at brain-based teaching* (2nd ed.). Thousand Oaks, CA: Corwin Press.

Stecher, B., & Barron, S. (2001, October). Unintended consequences of test-based accountability when testing in "milepost" grades. *Educational Assessment, 7*(4), 259–281.

Steele, C. (2004, May 3). Not just a test. *The Nation. New York, 278*(17), 38–41.

Strümpfer, D. J. W. (2003, May). Resilience and burnout: A stitch that could save nine. *South African Journal of Psychology, 33*(2), 69–79.

Suicide trends among youths and young adults aged 10–24 years-United States, 1990–2004 [Telebriefing]. (2007, September 6). Centers for Disease Control and Prevention.

Sunderman, G., Tracey, C., & Orfield, G. (2004, September). *Listening to teachers: Classroom realities and No Child Left Behind*. Retrieved September 2, 2004, from harvardscience.harvard.edu/directory/programs/civil-rights-project

Sylwester, R. (1995). *A celebration of neurons.* Alexandria, VA: Association for Supervision and Curriculum Development.

Sylwester, R. (2007) *The adolescent brain.* Thousand Oaks, CA: Corwin Press.

Tate, M. (2006). Learning styles. In S. Feinstein (Ed.), *The Praeger Handbook of Learning and the Brain* (Vol. 1, pp. 286–289). Westport, CT: Praeger.

Taylor, G., Shepard, L., Kinner, F., & Rosenthal, J. (2003). *A survey of teachers' perspectives on high-stakes testing in Colorado: What gets taught, what gets lost.* (CSE Technical Report 588). Retrieved October 3, 2004, from University of Colorado, Center for Research on Evaluation, Standards, and Student Testing Web site: http://education.colorado.edu/faculty/welnerk/Taylor.pdf

Thomas, P. L. (2001). Standards, standards everywhere, and not a spot to think. *English Journal, 91*(1) 63–67. Retrieved April 8, 2003, from ProQuest database.

Vandevoort, L. (2004, June). *National Board certified teachers and their students' achievement.* Tempe, AZ: Arizona State University.

Weissbourd, R. (2003, March). Moral teachers, moral students. *Educational Leadership, 60*(6), 6–11.

Wolfe, Pat. (2001*). Brain matters: Translating the research to classroom practice.* Alexandria, VA: ASCD.

Zull, J. E. (2004, September). The art of changing the brain. *Educational Leadership 62*(1).

Index

Note: Entries followed by *(t)* represent a table. Entries followed by *(f)* represent a figure. Entries followed by *(r)* represent a rubric.